Praise for Diana Athill and *Alive, Alive Oh!*

"Enchanting. . . . Diana Athill, 98, still has a few things to teach us about growing old with dignity and humor and grace."

—Associated Press

"[Athill] writes as a person of wide-ranging learning, a generalist, a lover of men and animals and a garden enthusiast, a person intoxicated with life." —*New York Times Book Review*

"To paraphrase Shakespeare, wisdom is bred in neither the heart nor the head, but in the bones that carry us through the decades. A few very talented artists, like Diana Athill, may persuade their old bones to yield up a glimpse or two of what they've learned." —*Salon*

"Supple, frank, unafraid of contradictions, [Athill's] literary voice has all the courageous intelligence one associates with a certain type of British writer but none of the chill."

—*The New Yorker*

"[Athill] evokes another grande dame of British letters in her uninhibited lifestyle and no-holds-barred, clarion voice . . . Doris Lessing." —*San Francisco Chronicle*

"[Athill] offers clear-eyed wisdom of the grandma-you-wish-you'd-had variety."

—*People*

"Beautifully written and exquisitely detailed . . . [Athill] mines her memories of a life well-lived and generously lays them out on the page for the rest of the world to enjoy."

—*Minneapolis Star Tribune*

"Inspired. . . . Athill's signature is precise, crisp phrasing of the kind that has the reader scrabbling for something with which to underline it." —*Guardian*

"A selective drift through memories before sleep. . . . [Athill's] writing favors precision and clarity and poise."
—*Guardian Weekly*

"A book infused with joie de vivre." —*Independent*

"There are . . . many treasures in this heterogeneous cabinet of curiosities." —*Financial Times*

"Each chapter is like a shard of light falling on a random corner of her past . . . her description of life in a grand house makes *Downton Abbey* feel shabby." —*Times* (London)

"Simultaneously brief and abundant, earthy and spiritual."
—*Sunday Telegraph*

"It is immediately clear that age has not withered [Athill's] ability to recall in pin-sharp detail her glorious Bohemian-literary past." —*Irish Mail on Sunday*

"At the age of 98, [Athill] is still wholeheartedly engaged with the world, as this candid collection of essays reveals."
—*Psychologies*

Alive, Alive Oh!

ALSO BY DIANA ATHILL

Fiction

An Unavoidable Delay

Don't Look at Me Like That

Memoirs

Stet

After a Funeral

Make Believe

Yesterday Morning

Somewhere Towards the End

Life Class (omnibus)

Letters

Instead of a Book

Alive, Alive Oh!

And Other Things That Matter

DIANA ATHILL

W. W. NORTON & COMPANY
Independent Publishers Since 1923
New York • London

For Phil and Annabel, with love
and endless gratitude

First published in Great Britain by Granta Publications

Printed in the United States of America
First published as a Norton paperback 2017

For information about permission to reproduce selections from this book, write to
Permissions, W. W. Norton & Company, Inc., 500 Fifth Avenue, New York, NY 10110

For information about special discounts for bulk purchases, please contact
W. W. Norton Special Sales at specialsales@wwnorton.com or 800-233-4830

Manufacturing by Quad Graphics, Fairfield

Library of Congress Cataloging-in-Publication Data

Names: Athill, Diana, author.
Title: Alive, alive oh! and other things that matter / Diana Athill.
Description: First American edition. | New York : W. W. Norton & Company, 2016. |
"First published in Great Britain by Granta Publications" [2015] — Verso title page.
Identifiers: LCCN 2015042206 | ISBN 9780393253719 (hardcover)
Subjects: LCSH: Athill, Diana. | Women authors, English—20th century—Biography. |
Authors, English—20th century—Biography. | Women editors—Great Britain—Biography. |
Editors—Great Britain—Biography. | Aging. | Old age. | Life. | Memory in old age.
Classification: LCC PR6051.T43 Z463 2016 | DDC 828/.91409—dc23
LC record available at http://lccn.loc.gov/2015042206

ISBN 978-0-393-35356-3 pbk.

W. W. Norton & Company, Inc.,
500 Fifth Avenue, New York, NY 10110
www.wwnorton.com

W. W. Norton & Company Ltd.,
15 Carlisle Street, London W1D 3BS

1 2 3 4 5 6 7 8 9 0

Contents

Introduction

'Sometimes I sits and thinks and sometimes I just sits': I have forgotten who it is who is supposed to have said that, but it is a good description of a state quite often observed in a retirement home, and considered pitiable. Disconcertingly, I recently realized that I myself (not often, just now and then) might say those very words if someone asked me what I was doing. It is not a welcome thought, but less dreadful than it might be because I now know from experience that the state is not necessarily pitiable at all. It is even rather pleasant – or it can be. That probably depends on the nature of the person sitting. To me it has been, because the thinking turns out to be about events in the past which were enjoyable, and when my mind relaxes itself it is those same events which float in and out of it.

Until about two months ago, those events included people, usually men. I talked about it the other day with someone who is also in her nineties, though not so far into them as I am, and she said, 'Yes, of course, men. What I do when I'm waiting to fall asleep is run through all the men I ever went to bed with,' whereupon we both laughed in a ribald way, because that is exactly what I did too. It cheered me up to learn that I had not been alone in indulging in this foolishness.

But then something odd happened. The things floating out of the past did often still include events which involved men, but just as often, and just as pleasurably, they were images of places and objects: all the most beautiful places and things that I once experienced.

About halfway through my seventies I stopped thinking of myself as a sexual being, and after a short period of shock at the fact, found it very restful. To be able to like, even to love, a man without wanting to go to bed with him turned out to be a new sort of freedom. This realization was extraordinary. It was like coming out onto a high plateau, into clear, fresh air, far above the antlike bustle going on down below me. It was almost like becoming another sort of creature. Well, I had in fact become another sort of creature: I had become an Old Woman! And to my surprise, I don't regret it. In the course of the ninety-seven years through which I have lived I have collected many more images of beautiful places and things than I realized, and now it seems as though they are jostling to float into my mind.

For example: because (I suppose) it will soon be May, I have just caught the scent of bluebells in my room. Once a booksellers' conference took me and some colleagues to Yorkshire, near Fountain's Abbey. An energetic colleague said to me, 'Let's get the hotel to call us at 5 o'clock tomorrow morning, so that we can nip out and have a good look at the Abbey before the day begins.' Never an early riser, I was at first appalled, then felt ashamed of myself and agreed, so we did it, and the Abbey was indeed very lovely, standing there in the silent and delicate mistiness of an early morning in May; but even more magical was the nearby woodland sloping down to the river, carpeted with bluebells which were responding to the rising sun by releasing a great wave of scent – a wave more powerful than I'd known their flowers could possibly produce. The little new leaves on the branches above them were that first green, which looks as though made by light, and which will be gone in a day or two, and blackbirds had just started to sing. Those few minutes in that wood were so piercingly beautiful that I ought not to be surprised at their still being with me.

Venice is the source of many more such memories – the special greenness of its water, the way rippling reflections pattern its walls, facade after facade, painting after painting that stop one in one's track – oh, how hopeless it is to try to put paintings into words. There are so many paintings which turn the 'I' into 'eye', take you right out of consciousness of self, and make you see, when you leave their presence, that everything has become more alive. All of Italy always seems to be waiting there to overwhelm me with its acute pleasures, so that dismal news of its political squalor becomes unbearable – although I'm sure that if I were able to go there again, my tourist-eye view of it would soon obliterate all but its art, its architecture, its olive trees, its cypresses. And surely its food would still taste like it ought to taste?

Food: in Tobago, friends once drove me to a little almost-round bay where forest came right down to the water's edge, and there we swam and lay on the sand drinking rum and grapefruit juice (as my hostess said, all that fruit juice surely made it very good for you) until their motor boat came puttering into the bay piloted by the island's only happily sea-going man – Joe was his name – who had been fishing as he came, carrying with him a big black iron pot and a chest containing their collection of spices. On that island surrounded by fish-filled ocean most people ate nothing but salt-dried fish – you rarely saw a boat. My friends found that absurd, so discovered Joe, bought him the boat, and every evening jeeped down to the little jetty under their house to meet him, unload his catch, and drive it slowly up the hill while they announced the arrival of fresh fish by blowing a conch (such an ancient and mournful sound). And out of the darkness came silent women, to buy their very cheap and delicious suppers. Which, if they were anything like our lunch that day … No, they probably were a little less good, because much of that wonderful fragrance which came wafting along the beach from the crackling fire over which Joe was stirring the big black pot was the result of well-chosen spices. The fish he cooked for us was easily the most beautiful meal I have ever eaten. Or ever will eat (alas!).

Other beautiful things? Oh yes, the Folk Museum at Santa Fe. The words 'folk museum' bode ill, suggesting rough brown pottery, more worthy than seductive. But folk produce much that is not brown (the Rio carnival for example), and the stuff in this museum was collected from all over the world by a man of the theatre, a master of the art of Display, which makes it a splendiferous palace of colour and fantasy in which you are soon running mad in your attempt to see everything, and there is so much that it's impossible to do that but you end up feeling dizzy with joy. To go to Santa Fe without visiting that museum would be a grave mistake.

And closer to home, the landscaping at Kenwood, contrived by Repton, matured to match what must have been his dream, and perfectly preserved: an exquisite prospect of green parkland sweeping down to water with woodland beyond, and a graceful bridge precisely where it ought to be. No other city has a romantic landscape so lovely, still there to soothe the spirits of innumerable Londoners, including me.

Looking at things is never time wasted. If your children want to stand and stare, let them. When I was marvelling at the beauty of a painting or enjoying a great view it did not occur to me that the experience, however intense, would be of value many years later. But there it has remained, tucked away in hidden bits of my mind, and now out it comes, shouldering aside even the most passionate love affairs and the most satisfying achievements, to make a very old woman's idle days pleasant instead of boring. And giving me this book, of memories, thoughts and reflections, which does – roughly – add up to being a report on what living for ninety-seven years has taught one rather lucky old woman.

April 2015

Highgate, London

My Grandparents' Garden

Ditchingham Hall, to which this garden belongs, is in Norfolk: an early Georgian house of red brick, which was bought by my great-grandfather and enlarged by my grandfather, who reactivated the old kiln where the bricks for the house had been made. Georgian bricks were smaller than modern ones. Gramps had the bricks for the extension of the house made the same size as the old ones, as well as of the same clay, so the join between old and new, still perceptible if you knew where to look when I was a child, has now become invisible. The house looks exactly as though it was originally built the size it now is.

When I was a child, in the 1920s and 1930s, the garden was looked after by scrawny, bearded Mr Wiseman – so like Beatrix Potter's Mr McGregor that they might have been brothers – with two men under him. It was large, much of it sloping slightly down from the house (more steeply so towards the lake), and it didn't exist only for ornamental purposes, but also to support the house. As well as lawns, shrubberies and a rose-garden there were stables, barns, pigsties, potting sheds and glasshouses. Because it was a pre-Jekyll garden, the rose beds were the only flower beds except for those for picking, tucked away in the kitchen garden. The glasshouses were the vinery, the nectarine house, the melon and cucumber house, and the big one full of colour, which was called Gran's greenhouse and was for the flowers in pots which came into the drawing room. And there may have been another small one behind Gran's, presumably for propagation.

The parts of the garden were distinct. There was the terrace with its view over the front park and lake, onto which the library opened from a door which used to be the house's front door before my grandfather changed things round. The terrace felt more like house than garden because one stepped out onto it so easily, and after breakfast Gran used to sit on its stone steps while she brushed Lola, her poodle. It was a place for civilized behaviour, where we interacted with our grown-ups more than in most places. The urns that stood at intervals on its wall had been brought back from Italy by Gramps, and small pink roses, with a lot of heavily scented honeysuckle, clambered over the walls – on summer evenings, through the bedroom windows overlooking the terrace there used to come delicious waves of honeysuckle. At one corner of the terrace a path led off along the side of the house to the big shrubbery that sloped down to the stackyard, where the outdoor privy intended for the men servants was concealed. After breakfast Gramps would tuck *The*

Times under his arm and proceed in a stately way to that privy, which he happened to prefer at that time of day, and if you noticed him going past a window you must pretend you hadn't. (I'm not sure if that is a memory of my own or one handed down by a cousin six years older than I am who knew things from before I was born.) At the terrace's other end, round the corner on the gravel sweep leading to the front door, was the cedar tree. There were other cedars, but this was *the* cedar tree, magnificent and surely everlasting, which gave the house's front view its beauty. (Of course nothing is 'everlasting'. Eventually the cedar's roots began to threaten the house's stability, so it had to go.)

Beyond the gravel stretched the lawns, the area for hospitality, which included the Mound, an oddly unnecessary little Edwardian feature which small children liked to roll down, but which had no other conceivable purpose, and, opposite the front door, the tennis courts, with two handsome cedars beyond and the Spreading Tree on the far right. The Spreading Tree must have been a very early Victorian, or perhaps even Georgian, folly – it was a larch, with a trunk stout enough to indicate considerable age. At the height of a tall man it had been fiercely trained to grow sideways in all directions (how this was done, God knows), supported where necessary by posts, so that it had ended up looking like a large, feathery green table, perfect for climbing into because its flattened and intertwined branches provided several comfortable hammocky places where you could lie reading, unseen by anything but a passing bird.

The lawn tapered off to the right, separated from the park by inconspicuous iron railings. Nowadays there is a beautiful herbaceous border between the lawn and the shrubbery, but in my childhood there was a gravel path, with a summer house tucked into the shrubbery and Gran's rose garden on the lawn side. The rose garden consisted of six, or perhaps eight, long narrow beds, each containing a different kind of tea rose, with between them pillars swathed in climbing roses. The rose garden was the place where Gran, who knew a great deal about gardening, actually got her hands on it. Near a back door of the house was a small room called the Flower Room because vases were kept and flowers were arranged there (and wet dogs were dried off). In it Gran kept her leather gauntlets, secateurs, trowel and a big watering can with a long brass syringe. At the first sight of a greenfly that can was filled with a mixture of water and soft soap, and out she went to give the roses a good drench. No chemical ever touched them, and they were always radiantly healthy. I think Gran pruned them, too – all her daughters grew up to be skilled pruners.

The part of the shrubbery next to the Mound was shaded by a tree as splendid in its way as *the* cedar: a glorious great beech. Beeches, alas, are comparatively short-lived trees. Many of them were planted in the park and garden, all at the same time during the eighteenth century when the grounds were first laid out, and they really were the glory of the park (though no individual tree was more splendid than this one, so near the house) . . . and now: all gone, not because of anyone's decision, just because of their age. We used to have tea under that tree, and once we acted a play there, the first play I ever was in. I think I was a mushroom – not a speaking part, so I can't have forgotten my lines, but I do have a dim sad little memory of having to be forgiven for getting something wrong – perhaps the mushroom had hopped about. Which didn't prevent me from loving that tree so much that a few years later I stood underneath it trying passionately to will my ghost to haunt that place after I was dead.

My grandfather's extension of the house had made its ground-plan U-shaped instead of square. Every spring six big pots of fuchsias were set out in the space between the wings. The back door of the original house was never used. 'Our' back door was in the wing on the left (as you looked back at the house). Beside it were hung mackintoshes and several hooded loden cloaks, which could be used by anyone, as could the several pairs of 'jemimas' standing in a row beneath them. Jemimas, which I've never seen or heard of elsewhere, were clumsy overshoes made of waterproofed felt, fastening over the instep with a latchet. Galoshes were considered sissy, whereas jemimas, although they looked much more old-womanish, were perfectly acceptable on manly feet. The last door into the house in the other wing led into the laundry, which once a week became a quite alarming steamy hell when an old woman called Mrs Rayner came to do the house's washing in an enormous copper. Some of it was hung to dry on racks on the floor above the copper, but most of it dried on the bleach, which was a feature of most large houses.

The bleach was a grassy space slightly larger than a tennis court where linen was hung or spread to be whitened by sunlight. Ours was sheltered from the wide gravel way down to the stables by a tall and solid yew hedge. At the bleach's end were the kennels, so-called in spite of the fact that no dog was ever kept in them. When my cousin Pen and I were respectively about twelve and ten, we kept our goats in the kennels, or rather we milked them and put them to bed there. All day they were tethered out of doors in places carefully chosen by us for their lushness. We had goats because I was supposed for a time to be consumptive, or nearly so (a false alarm), and cow's milk was thought to be the cause of it, which it well might have been in those days. The scare was one for which I was grateful: because of it I spent a whole year living with Gran rather than just visiting her frequently as the rest of the family did. Living there, and not having to do lessons: my idea of pure heaven, and at that age a year seems like for ever. Apart from a few setbacks, I have been lucky all my life, and that unforgettable year was the start of it.

The stables came next – or rather the top stables, built of the same brick as the house, and sedately overlooking a small lawn round which the back drive swirled. The first door into the stables led to the room where the house's electricity was made, too mystifying to be familiar. Next came the harness room, Seeley's stronghold. He had been my great-grandfather's coachman, so he went on being called coachman rather than groom all his life. When my great-grandparents came to Norfolk from

Yorkshire, Seeley rode the two grey carriage horses all the way down, so I suppose my great-grandmother's brougham must have been purchased after the move. There were two stalls and one big loose box in the stable, the big box being Susan's. She was the smart little black hackney mare who pulled Gramps's dog cart and covered the twelve miles to Norwich within an hour. When they reached Norwich Gramps would stop at a respectable pub on its outskirts, where Susan was well looked after while he walked about his business in the city. The two stalls were usually inhabited by hunters belonging to my uncle who came and went complete with their own groom. The last part of the stables was the coach house, which quite soon became the garage, where the chauffeur, Mr Youngman, cherished my grandparents' boringly sober car. (Youngman, with his wife and daughters, lived in a cottage which had a plaster cherub above its front door, which for some time my brother and I thought was Mr Youngman as a baby.)

Our ponies, when not out to grass as they mostly were, lived in the lower stables. Since both Pen and I, and later my sister Patience, were horse-mad, these were important. There was a steep drop at that point, so we reached the lower stables either by a flight of steps at the corner of the bleach, or by the back drive which circled down to it round a grassy hillock on which there grew a handsome walnut tree. Backing onto the top stables there was a row of smaller loose boxes, each with a half-door, looking out onto a rough square. On the left there was a large coach house where the dog carts were kept (later assorted cars). Opposite there was a big black barn where for a long time Great-granny's brougham and the wagonette slowly mouldered away under ever-thickening layers of dust, and the governess cart, still often used by us, stood by Uncle Bill's goat cart. I was familiar with a photograph of Bill as a little boy proudly driving his goat, but never saw the cart in use. The fourth side of the square was occupied by a row of low buildings for keeping things in, only one of which was special: the one in which every year Seeley cured the ham – the pigsty, by the way, was attached to the end of the barn, and if you were me you were careful to avoid the lower yard on the dreadful day when the annual pig was killed. Seeley, a good Yorkshireman, knew the secrets of curing a ham in the proper Yorkshire way, and after the pig-killing there would be several days when he abandoned the stables, retreated to one of these little houses, and became almost priestly in devotion to his grave task. You must not disturb him, though you could peep. Usually he was very ready to talk, full of fascinating horse information. (One white foot, buy a horse / Two white feet, try a horse / Three white feet, look well about him / Four white feet, do without him.) Seeley's hams were wonderful. There was always one on the sideboard at breakfast time, and if anyone was foolish enough when carving it to 'scoop' it in a misguided attempt to avoid fat, Gramps became very cross indeed. (Those breakfasts! As well as the ham there was always a boiled egg each for every person there, as well as the main dish – perhaps sausages and bacon, or grilled kidneys. And quite often no one ate a boiled egg. What on earth happened to them? A present-day kind of solution such as eggs mayonnaise for supper would certainly have had no place in Mrs Wiseman's kitchen. Mrs Wiseman, by the way, was Wiseman's daughter, not his wife. The 'Mrs' was an honorary title always given to cooks. In spite of all that food no one was fat, I suppose because we walked and rode so much.)

Alongside the drive leading down to the lower stable yard there was a tall beech hedge, looking at first sight like the garden's end. It was in fact the beginning of the most important part of it: the kitchen garden. Just through the gate in the hedge there was on the left an apple orchard and on the right a rather disorderly space containing the aviary in which Gran's ringdoves lived, the big frame in which her parma violets were grown, the melon and cucumber house, and in the background (I think) various kinds of manure and compost heaps. The parma violet frame was impressive. I suppose they are not easy to cultivate (one never sees them nowadays), but Mr Wiseman was clearly an expert: the intensely fragrant flowers were large and grew profusely for what seemed like the whole year. They were Gran's favourites. Beside her chair in the drawing room there was always a silver bowl full of them. It can't really have been there all through the year, but it is impossible to picture her sitting there without it . . . and any violet I have sniffed at since then has been a sad disappointment.

Once you were past the melon house you came to the walled garden proper, with the other greenhouses and the long, low potting shed on your right, which was always in perfect order and, unlike most modern potting sheds, contained no chemicals except for a small sack of Epsom salts. Muck, leaf mould and the hoe: those were Mr Wiseman's weapons (with, of course, other hands to wield the hoe; its chip-chip-chip was almost always to be heard). In the eighteenth century William Cobbett wrote a didactic book about gardening which included a plan of the ideal kitchen garden. Many years after I had grown up and was living in London, I came across it, and to my delight recognized the Ditchingham kitchen garden in every detail; except that where we had the melon house, he had a most elaborately composed 'hot bed' on which to grow melons. The Ditchingham garden had quite obviously been laid out according to the instructions in his book, with that one improvement added.

It was walled on three sides, the fourth being sheltered by the apple orchard and the large cage for soft fruit, where the raspberries, strawberries and currants could flourish, protected from birds. A stream bisected the garden. Before the stream came through the left-hand wall, and after it went out through the right-hand wall, it was just a large ditch with water at its bottom between rough grassy banks. For the width of the garden it was a smooth little canal, full to the brim between brick banks. This was achieved by a weir at the point where it left the garden, which controlled the water's flow to the exact extent that produced a full canal and a gentle outflow over the weir. The canal was crossed at three places by little iron bridges – the bridge nearest the weir had a plank bridge beside it, the purpose of which I don't know, although it was certainly more comfortable than its iron neighbour to sit on, with feet dangling in the water, during our many tadpole and newt fishing sessions. On one side of the canal was a wide herbaceous border, handsome although it was there only for picking, as were the sweet peas. The rest of the walled garden was devoted to exquisitely grown vegetables, and the walls to espaliered fruit.

A well-cultivated walled kitchen garden is beautiful. It has a peculiar serenity derived from its purpose, not unlike that of a church, which you feel as soon as you enter it . . . or rather, that was how it used to be, when its purpose, the sustaining of a household, was real. For a good many years now, that purpose has ceased to exist, wiped out by the patterns of modern living, so it is pointless to regret the fact that Ditchingham's kitchen garden has been replaced by a very lovely pleasure-garden; but I feel it a privilege to have known it while it was still fulfilling its original purpose, because it was – it really was – a wonderfully thought-out and maintained fabrication of great beauty. There was not a single part of it that did not function exactly as it was meant to.

That was no thanks to us, the children, though we did play our parts properly up to a point. There were certain things which we were supposed to do, and we did them. During summer, for instance, it was the custom that the women and children of the house picked the strawberries and raspberries that were to be eaten that day, collecting them into big, cool cabbage leaves, and they also picked the sweet peas, which had to be done regularly if they were to be kept flowering as long as possible. No hardship there – indeed, a good deal of pleasure, particularly among the raspberries, because there was no rule against nibbling as you went along. Strawberries were slightly less enjoyable because of the necessary stooping or squatting. Towards the end of the season it did become a bit of a chore, particularly with the sweet peas because their stalks became shorter and shorter, which made big fat bunches less rewarding, but I don't remember ever thinking of going on strike. However, although we didn't leave undone that which we ought to do, we did do a good many things we ought not to do, particularly Pen and me, who prided ourselves on being connoisseurs of peaches.

The peaches grew against the far wall (against which the vinery was built: it faced south so got the full benefit of the sun). Next to the peaches were the huge yellow pears greatly valued by Gramps, each of which would be wrapped in white muslin by Mr Wiseman to protect it from wasps. Pen and I never stole a pear because, I suppose, that muslin bestowed on them some kind of semi-magical untouchability, but we kept a sharp eye on the peaches, and struck as soon as they were ripe. There was a convenient little door in the wall near where they grew, leading into the Cedar Walk, the strip of ornamental woodland that girdled the kitchen garden and was the end of the garden as a whole, and having grabbed our chosen peaches we would dart out of the door into the Cedar Walk, where we could guzzle them in safety. 'I'll tell your granny on you!' Mr Wiseman would roar if he saw us, but it wasn't that threat which alarmed us because we knew how mild Gran's scolding would be; it was the force of Mr Wiseman's anger. To him we were pestilential little nuisances who deserved a good smacking, and we felt it.

Stealing the grapes was much harder. The vinery door was often left open to give them air, and there was a stepladder handy, but manoeuvring the ladder into place, climbing it, choosing the place in a bunch where the nipping-out of a grape would be least noticeable (taking a whole bunch was unthinkable) – all that made darting impossible, so we did it very rarely. And as far as I was concerned there was a slight impulse to be protective of the grapes, because Gran had taught me how to thin them. They, like the roses, gave her the chance to get her hands on her garden. If the bunches were to reach perfection, halfway through their ripening a good half of the grapes had to be cut out, so that none of those left touched a neighbour. The result looked terrible, poor skinny little bunches which must surely perish; but, 'No, no, don't stop,' Gran would urge, and of course she was right. The bunches when fully ripe were marvellously shapely groupings of big plump grapes, each one perfect within a perfect whole. It was hard to decide which was more delicious, the green or the purple. I think it was really the green, because they were true muscats, but the purple were so beautiful that one seemed to be tasting their appearance.

The other things we stole were not the figs, but gooseberries. The fig tree grew next to our escape door and bore a lot of fruit because, according to Gramps, it had been planted properly with a dead donkey under its roots; and it may have been the thought of that poor donkey that prevented me from liking figs very much until I was older. The gooseberries were in a second fruit cage at the edge of the lower orchard (cooking apples and quinces), which was outside the walls of the kitchen garden – a sort of overspill. There were little hard green gooseberries, good for cooking but very sharp uncooked, small round red ones which were pleasant enough, and very large golden ones which were sweet and succulent. Stealing those was boring because no one minded – they were not considered precious – but we did it quite often when the Golden Balls were at their best. Apart from them, the lower orchard offered no temptations, but one tree became, to me, special. When I reached my teens we lived for some years in the Hall Farm, just across the park from Gran's house, and walked back and forth between the two houses every day, often more than once, passing through that orchard every time. Close to the path, just before one crossed the stream to cut through a corner of the Cedar Walk into the back park, there was a very old apple tree which leaned over the path and bore huge emerald-green cooking apples. One day, as I stooped to go under its branches, I came face to face with a group of these apples, and for some reason was suddenly acutely aware of how amazing they were. I stood quite still, gazing at them – gazing and gazing. It was as though I could hear them Being, as though something must be about to happen because of them . . . I think it was the nearest I ever came to a mystical experience. It didn't happen again, but left me with a secret respect and affection for that tree – and may have been the beginning of a feeling that trees are as much living things as animals are, which I have to this day.

In the Cedar Walk, of course, the trees ruled. You entered it from that lower orchard, or from the kitchen garden, or from the back drive. At that end it was a dense, almost impenetrable mass of yew, laurel and box, but it allowed itself certain frivolities: beside the gate into it, for example, there were two sources of exceptionally sweet scent, a sweet briar and a syringa (nowadays we would call it a philadelphus), and you soon came to a neat little island of lawn at the centre of which there stood a tall and shapely red may tree, an elegant surprise. Opposite there was a sprawl of honey-scented yellow azaleas, and then a group of bamboos on the edge of the stream, where it was just about to slip under the wall and become the kitchen garden canal. Across the stream the Cedar Walk proper began, announced by two handsome beeches, one on either side of the broad, mossy path, and then came the cedars, spaced out beside the path – I can no longer remember how many of them, but think it was six or seven. Between them and the kitchen garden was a small forest of tall yew trees, not densely crowded together, but enough of them to produce a darkness, and on the other side of the path a narrow strip of shrubs and smaller trees separated the Walk from the park. Where it came to its orchard end there was a group of rhododendrons, a big holly tree, and a row of smaller beeches beside the stream, on one of which we had all carved our initials.

The Cedar Walk had been planned and planted by someone

who was never going to see it – not him, nor his children, nor even his children's children, though they would have had a clearer view of what it was going to be. What amazingly generous confidence in the future those eighteenth-century landscape designers had! By the time my great-grandfather bought the house their dream had become reality: there was this serene, sheltered, splendid walk where the ladies of the house could take healthy exercise without dirtying their shoes, and the gentlemen could retire to think their thoughts inspired by woodland privacy. (When during the Second World War the house was taken over by the Army, one of the officers who was there for a while told me that he imagined himself pacing that walk with a copy of Horace's *Odes* in his hands. Need I say that I fell in love with him.) We children, when we stalked each other, birds'-nested, climbed trees, dammed the stream or just idled in the Cedar Walk, were inhabiting a two-hundred-year-old dream: a place planned to support not only its inhabitants' bodies, but also their minds – perhaps even their souls. And we were too young to perceive how near that dream was to reaching its end. How profoundly lucky we were! And how lucky Ditchingham Hall has been to pass into hands that can steer it out of that disappearing dream into a life that belongs to the present.

There was a time, after my uncle's death, when it looked as though this was not going to happen. I remember walking in the park, looking at the empty house – it's extraordinary how heavily the emptiness of a house declares itself – and finding it painful beyond words. Not for anything would I have gone into the abandoned garden, and my mother and my uncle's other surviving sister could hardly bring themselves to think about what might be going to happen. The feeling was a strange one: not just regret that a lovely house might vanish, but a sense that all of our past lives that it had contained would vanish with it. Not a rational feeling on my part, given how far the realities of my life now were from anything to do with that place, but I was surprised at how powerful it was. It was a great relief when we learnt that my uncle's daughter and her husband had decided to move into the Hall: a far from light decision, given its size, and how much it needed modernizing. It was as though something in ourselves, not just the house, had come alive again.

All this reminds me of an absurdity. I think I was thirteen. For some unremembered reason I was alone in the back park on a lovely spring day, sprawling on the grass among daisies, wallowing in the feeling of how much I loved this place. If only it could one day be mine! And I began to wonder if that could ever happen. Disregarding tiresome matters such as income, and supposing inheritance within our family would follow the same pattern as inheritance in the royal family, who – I asked myself – would have to die before it came to me? My mother being my grandparents' youngest daughter, it soon became evident that it would be everyone, even my brother, because would he be likely to accept that I being older than him prevailed over his being male? Not a hope! He was as devoted to the place as I was, and even more ruthless. The whole lot of them would have to go except for my younger sister ... and would it be acceptable for me to pray for such a holocaust? No, of course it would not. So: it would never, never, never be mine, and that was that.

One of our unfortunate governesses used sometimes to exclaim in despair, 'Why, oh why, can't you behave like Rational Beings?' I think it was at that moment in the back park that rationality set in and began to replace daydreams with an appreciation of what I really owed, and still owe, to having spent so much of my youth in that dear place.

Post-War

It annoys me when someone describes this country in the late 1940s and 1950s as being dreary, an opinion usually based on the continuation of rationing for some years after the war's end. People who see it like that can't have lived through the war. Those of us still alive who did so see it differently.

I was twenty-one when the war began, twenty-seven when it ended, and during one's twenties a year is much longer – very much longer – than it is in later life (I can vouch for the fact that by the time you are in your late nineties it flashes by in a trice). It appears from the records that some of the men responsible for running the war sometimes envisaged us losing it, but I don't think many ordinary people did (God knows why not) and I'm sure I never did; but I did quite often feel that it was never going to end. Greyness, joylessness, sadness swerving in and out of despair, being forced endlessly to *endure*: all that had become what Life *was*. And I could see no end to it. Because I didn't want to stop being alive, I avoided as much as possible dwelling on this miserable condition, but that didn't stop me being in it. So when the war did in fact end, what I remember most clearly is standing in Piccadilly in a crowd of jubilant people, telling myself: 'You've got to believe it, you must make yourself believe it – IT'S OVER,' and realizing that that belief had not yet fully dawned.

That was on VE day (Victory in Europe). By VJ day (Victory in Japan) the wonderful truth of Overness was shining out, so much so that it blinded me to the horror of those bombs on Japan, and I was able to romp down the Mall with a group of friends to yell in wholehearted joy for the royals to come out on their balcony. The vast crowd gathered there was so benignly happy that there was no jostling or shoving, and although many people were forced to stand in the beds of geraniums in front of the palace, *The Times* next morning reported that none of the plants had been damaged. In spite of those Vs, it was not Victory that was being celebrated. It was *peace*, the return of Life to what it ought to be.

It is true that the return was slow, but how, after all that we had been through, could it have been otherwise? It would have been daft to expect speed. Much better to enjoy getting gradually better and better, getting more and more for each coupon in your ration book, knowing that before long you would be throwing that book away. It is true that on my first visit to Italy I did notice that shop windows in Florence were full of things still absent from shop windows in London (oh, those pastries!), and that the people of Florence were ahead of us in repairing bomb damage; but all I can remember feeling about that is how much I enjoyed what I was seeing. Everything was enjoyable *because I was abroad*, I was travelling, as I had lost hope of doing. 'But,' says gloompot, 'all you could take with you was a mere £25, the control of currency was so strict.' Yes, of course. But was it not astounding how much you could do on £25, particularly if you were young? I was already too old for sleeping on beaches or under haystacks, as my younger cousins did, but I could happily make do with the most modest *pensioni* or bed-and-breakfasts and thought nothing of sitting up all night in trains – had in fact some of the most marvellous holidays in my life, and could not have afforded to take more money with me if I'd been allowed it, so there was no hardship there.

The best adventure of the early fifties was the discovery of Club Méditerranée, just launched by the Belgian family Blitz. My cousin Barbara and I saw a little advertisement for a holiday in Corfu costing only £21, and decided to risk it. We had to get ourselves to Venice, where we would board a Greek ship, travelling steerage in a crowd of Club Med members, all of us equipped with long necklaces of white Pop It beads issued to us when we signed on, to be used instead of money when we reached Corfu. This simple but brilliant device added greatly to the holiday's charms, because (although we had paid for the beads in London) using them instead of coins felt so deliciously carefree. Every transaction at the Club's bar, or at the office where we booked excursions and so on, seemed as though it was free.

It was early enough in the Club's history for the accommodation to be in tents – yellow tents and orange tents, scattered quite far apart among the olive trees on a big estate – olive orchards and scrubby woodland, with islands of magnificent plane trees, one group sheltering the dining area, another the bar, a biscuit-toss from the water, where the water-skiing motor boats took off. The air smelt of herbs, at night the only sound was the strange cry of the little skops owls. Every need was catered for with inconspicuous ingenuity: for example, if you needed to iron a garment there was a power-point among the roots of one of the plane trees which had an ironing board propped against it with an iron attached.

Each time a batch of *gentils membres* (as they called us) arrived, they were given a little talk by the woman who ran the camp, a member of the Blitz family. We were welcomed charmingly and given information about the amenities, available excursions and so on, and then lectured rather sternly about how we should behave outside the Club's premises. Within them we were free to behave however we liked, but outside we must remember that we were guests of the Corfiots, who were unaccustomed to flocks of foreigners and had sensibilities of their own which it was essential to respect. So we must dress decently and avoid rowdy behaviour, and this was important. Barbara and I were favourably impressed by this talk – an opinion not shared by the only other English people in our group, a pair of young men. On that very evening they went out, got drunk at a local bar, stripped off their clothes and ran naked into the sea. Next day they were sent home. It has not been Club Med's fault if since then tourism in Corfu has become more louche.

The tents were all labelled with the names of their inhabitants, and Barbara and I were, at first, surprised at how many French people had double-barrelled names. The penny soon dropped. We, I think, were the only so-to-speak rogue women there; all the others were part of a couple, married or not. The place was staffed by young men hoping for a holiday in the sun, where they expected plenty of girls to be available. Few were, so we became perhaps over-valued by the staff. Barbara settled for a very handsome Corsican, who was a bit too macho to be easily managed; I for a rather older Belgian, good value there (he danced a mean tango), but a great bore when he turned up later in London. We confined these conquests to the evenings, when there was always dancing at the bar, because we wanted to see as much of Corfu as possible during the days. For that we picked up two very respectable middle-aged Corfiots, mine being the island's *chef de tourisme*, called (as so many Corfiots are) Spiridon, Spiro for short.

Spiro's job, he said, was difficult, because there was not as yet any money for it. He had, however, been able to buy four little cypress trees which he had just planted in such a way that when fully grown they would most gracefully frame a particularly beautiful view. He drove us to see these little trees, and to help us envisage the lovely effect they would eventually have. It would indeed have been deplorable to offend dear Spiro's sensibilities.

While this holiday made us admire Belgian efficiency and good taste, it had a sad effect on our opinion of the French, who were the majority of the Club members. On the ship from Venice we had eaten one supper. Being a Greek ship, it served Greek food, and since we were steerage passengers it was cheap Greek food: rather tough meat, a salad of roughly chopped-up cucumber and tomatoes, and rice pudding with dollops of jam ... and oh, the moans and groans and even vomiting noises with which this meal was greeted by our French companions; they might have been offered dishes of pigswill. Thank God, they told each other, that soon they'd be in the camp where, they had been promised by the Club's promotion booklet, they would be reunited with *cuisine française*.

Cut to our first meal in the camp's open-air dining space. Corfu being a Greek island, the food, not surprisingly, was Greek food, and given the large numbers catered for daily, cheap Greek food: rather tough meat, a salad of roughly chopped-up cucumber and tomatoes and rice pudding with dollops of jam. *And they fell on it with cries of joy.* So much, we felt, for the French's reputation as sophisticated foodies. And their manners were pretty crude, too. Each table seated eight people and at its centre was a big dish piled with chunks of bread. If the bread ran out you could ask for more, so why, every mealtime, was there a scuffle as people tried to be the first at their table so that they could pile many chunks of bread on their side plates? But though dining was a bit primitive, the bar made up for it, by providing the most exquisite *citrons pressés*. There was, of course, plenty of alcohol as well, but for us, who hadn't set eyes on a lemon for years, that was what we most enjoyed.

The only disappointment in that holiday was that neither of us was any good at water-skiing. How lovely to be one of the people skimming so gracefully over the sea, and how mortifying that neither of us ever stayed upright on that bloody board for more than a few seconds. Perhaps we would have mastered it given time, but there were always people lounging about, waiting their turn, so embarrassment made us give up.

Perhaps my fondest memory of the place is of the afternoon when, feeling unsociable, I took a book and a blanket for lying on to a tiny hidden beach far from the tents, which was so lovely and peaceful that it was seducing me from my book, when crunch, crunch: slow – furtive? – footsteps approached through the bushes, betrayed by the dryness and brittleness of the grass and leaves underfoot. Oh no! I thought, sitting up furiously. There was no one there. Had I imagined it? I lay down again. Crunch, crunch. This time I stood up. Still no one. Till another crunch drew my eyes down, and there was a large tortoise labouring his way through the grass towards the water.

I've never been to a modern Club Med, which would be, I gather, very much more glossy, but I still think of the organization fondly. To me it means that tortoise, the voice of the skops owl, the scent of sun-baked herbs, Spiro's trees, moonlit tangos, and those *citrons pressés*. It all seemed the very essence of Life returned to what it ought to be.

At home, too, that feeling prevailed; and it embraced a sense that we could make it *more* like it ought to be than it was before the war. In the 1930s middle- and upper-class people had been having a very good time, but many of them had felt at least a little guilty about the ugly rift between the haves and the have-nots. The young people I knew when I was up at Oxford were all (apart from a few with scholarships) benefiting from their parents' politics, but none of them was in sympathy with those politics. Many of us, including me, felt we ought to join the Communist Party, and some of us did. The reason why I was not among them was not worthy of respect. I did feel uneasy about ends justifying means, which I understood should be believed by a good Communist, but I held back mostly because of laziness. It seemed to me that devotion to the cause would be hard work and leave little time for the pleasant frivolities which I was enjoying so much.

Obviously if we, the privileged, had been feeling twinges of guilt, the many underprivileged were seething. The country was, in fact, in a bad way. Therefore it was not surprising that the election immediately after the war's end was won by the Labour Party. I was working at the BBC, in a humble part of it: the information library attached to the news room for the World Service. We all stayed up all night in the news room, listening to the results coming in and getting happier and happier, because they were what everyone in that room wanted. None of us questioned

Churchill's importance as our wartime leader, but none wanted the old man to steer us back into the past. It is sad to remember how sure we were that we could now set about building a good future in which fairness and justice would reign at home while we ceased to profit from our overseas 'possessions', having 'given' them their freedom to go their own ways. Yes, it is certainly sad now, given where we are and what we have become; but it was happy to live through at the time.

And there were genuine good things ahead, the NHS for one. We were soon taking it for granted and now spend more time lamenting its shortcomings than acknowledging its achievements, but to anyone who remembers medicine before the war it remains an almost miraculous institution – the one huge, solid gain achieved by our society that we must hang on to whatever else we lose. Education, too, leapt ahead. It still leaves much to be desired, but it is immensely better than it was pre-war. And the standard of living rose. Many people on very low incomes began to join the rest of us by taking for granted indoor toilets, refrigerators, and other household comforts ... which makes our present dive into poverty horrifying. During those 'dreary' years we got so used to simple, material things getting better that their getting worse now seems to be against nature.

In middle-class life those years sparkled in many ways. Fashion came alive again dramatically when Dior's New Look crossed the Channel. During the seemingly endless war years we had been stuck with square shoulders, straight up-and-down silhouettes and hems a few inches below the knee. Now, suddenly, we could look feminine again, and embark on the delightful journey of sudden absurd changes (colours were constantly being called 'the new black') that turn the necessity of clothing the body into fun. And just as enlivening as the new styles of dress were those in design generally. It became a matter of great interest in every field. Before the war the smartest look in the furnishing and decoration of houses was all-over whiteness, and the most common was cream-coloured walls cheered up by flowery chintz curtains and chair covers. Now, if walls weren't orange they were covered with adventurous wallpaper. I can't remember the exact date of a wallpaper exhibition at (I suppose) the new Design Centre, but I can vividly remember how enchanted I was by it. I managed somehow to scrape together the money to paper the walls of my bedroom (how? The BBC was paying me £380 a year) and I had it done in ivy – life-sized ivy leaves swarmed from floor to ceiling on all four walls (luckily I wasn't bold enough to put different patterns on each wall, which became quite the thing). I was tremendously pleased with it and it was hideous. I hadn't the faintest idea of how to decorate a room successfully. I see now that this was not because I had no eye for good furniture and pictures, but because the house I had known and loved best as a child, my maternal grandparents' in Norfolk, although not furnished quite as grandly as the houses regularly featured in *Country Life*, was in that style. That house, that magazine, museums and picture galleries: it was those that had formed my taste. Given a Greek shipping millionaire as a husband (or perhaps even better, as a lover) I could have done my drawing room beautifully, with ravishing pieces of eighteenth-century furniture, fine Persian rugs and truly good paintings, but it didn't even occur to me that someone with very little money could make a room look pretty. I just managed with bits of stuff my parents had let me take from home and the occasional object, however unsuitable, that had caught my eye. I was nearly sixty before I made a room look (I hope) attractive.

I didn't see anything of the official celebrations – the Festival of Britain, organized in celebration of the New Elizabethan Age, as it was called. This was partly because, having left the BBC not long after peace returned, I was soon very busy helping to launch a new publishing firm, and more because I had no man to do things with, being at that time between two love affairs.

Later, when the sixties began, most people frothed with excitement about them. To me they appeared to be just a continuation of the good times following the bad ones, and I was too contented to take much notice of the development of the Cold War. I knew, of course, that it was generally considered threatening, but I remembered what real 'threatening' had felt like in 1939, when everyone knew in their bones what was coming (the surge of relief felt when the Prime Minister returned from a visit to Hitler and announced that we could expect 'peace for our time' had been no more than superficial). Sniffing the air during the various post-war crises, I could detect no whiff of that threat, whatever was going on in foreign affairs. But although my instinct about that happened to be right, I was no more aware than anyone else of what was really going on in this country after the war.

This was not surprising, because the process seemed to be as slow, and thus imperceptible, as the shifting of tectonic plates which change the nature of the planet, although in fact it was very much faster than that. If people had paid more attention to history they would have remembered that it doesn't take long for an empire to collapse. When I was a child I used to pore over an atlas, deriving much satisfaction from how much of the world was coloured pink, which meant, they told me, that it was ours. I pitied other countries with their little patches of inferior colours, and I suspect that when a personal misfortune in my early twenties gave my confidence a nasty shock, that childhood schooling in feeling proud contributed a good deal to my recovery. It went deep, that feeling that we, the British, were Great: deeper, it turned out, in a lot of other people than it did in me, because it would not be long before I grew out of it, and by the time I went to university I had become sure that we ought to be giving all our pinkness back to its real owners. But, being ignorant of economics, I was unaware that this would mean our having to change our nature – an ignorance which appears to be true of our politicians to this day. The difference between being at the hub of a vast empire and being a tiny island off the shores of, but not belonging to, Europe seems to be something they are unable to understand. Their attempts to become European indicate awareness of a problem, but the blundering reluctance of those attempts – an apparent feeling that Europe ought to be grateful for our condescension in joining it – makes it clear how superficial these attempts are. Perhaps the task of making our island work well simply *as such* is actually impossible, and we will have to settle for being a tax haven for the rich of other countries? (I am glad that I shall be dead before the answer to that question becomes clear.) But although it is probably tragic that the people running our country in the years immediately after the war knew no better than ignorant citizens such as me what was beginning to happen to no-longer-great Britain, and what to do about it, it remains true that while they were going on, those were lovely years to live through.

'Oh, tell me, Gentle Shepherd, where . . .'

Thoughts on the attempted revolution in Trinidad and Tobago

The pelicans circled all morning, lifting and sinking on air currents, but always at more or less the same height above the silky sea. They looked aimless, but they were not. Every minute or so one of them saw what it was looking for, and the gimlet-twist with which it stabbed down into the water was so swift that surely the bird must pierce right to the bottom, disappearing for a long time. Instead, the splash had hardly settled before it was bobbing duck-like on the surface, gulping its catch. I liked watching them because the presence of creatures which at home were seen only in zoos was delightful proof that I really had arrived, at last, in a faraway and long-imagined place.

The birds didn't scream or squawk as fishing gulls would have done and their silence increased awareness of the greater silence. Insects chirred and creaked, of course, but so constantly that they stopped being heard. The tiny yellow and black sugarbirds chittered and fidgeted in the bush of their choice, but that was a sound so slight that it mingled with the insects'. A hummingbird's presence was noticed only because a flower trembled. At other times of day there were frogs, some of them sounding like birds, and birds, some of them sounding like frogs, but in mid-morning the silence of the sea surrounding Tobago seemed to flow right over the island. Even in the villages people's voices, cocks crowing and dogs barking, donkeys braying and boys practising – plink plonk – on a pan slung from a mango branch would not have registered so distinctly were it not for the silence. Cars were heard approaching a long way off and at nightfall, when the few fishing boats came in and their catch was being driven round the neighbourhood, the sound of the conch which summoned customers – a sea cow lowing mournfully for its lost calf – was like an important event.

The silence was only one of many pleasures. The heat might not count as a pleasure in some circumstances – one was drenched in sweat at the least agitation, to say nothing of exertion – but when activity is a matter of lazy choice, as it was for a visitor, heat becomes a luxury, and so is being physically untrammelled: the constrictions of underclothes, stockings, shoes are taken for granted until they are shed, but being rid of them is delicious.

In this tropical place the body enjoyed freedom, and so did the mind. There was so much to look at that the 'I' could forget itself, which left the feeling of a full day passing quickly, but was profoundly restful.

The sea might be the eye's main joy – but its beauty doesn't surprise. You know beforehand that the Caribbean will be blue and green like liquid jewels, and sometimes (when it lies shallow over white coral sand) lambent, as though light were shining up through it. Its beauty is recognized, not discovered, belonging as it does to a recent public dream of the place in which only its beaches exist. To me it seemed astonishing that I should be in this dream, but not astonishing that it was there.

The mountains and the forests, on the other hand, belong to a different and far older dream.

The plunging valleys jostle with leaves like open hands, like elephants' ears, like saws, like feathers, like fans, like frayed wickerwork. Flowers clamber and perch as though they had claws and wings. Birds are secretive but unafraid (this is not a place where men have preyed on birds). At the bottom of valleys run streams hidden by dark arches of bamboos, and the sound of water makes it seem cool even though there is more moisture than chill in the air. Cascades. Pools. A zigzag drift of butterflies. Small snappings and patterings, mysterious creakings. Fear? The tangle of green is so rampageous, the air is so heavy ... But there are no dangerous animals on Tobago, no poisonous snakes (two kinds of those on nearby Trinidad but none here). Stand quietly, reminding yourself that this forest won't hurt you, and fear fades. You can walk further into it, following one of the many traces. You can get to know it.

Any botanist or ornithologist would be drunk with excitement in five minutes. My ignorant eye was drunk with beauty and strangeness – and with a dizzy sensation that the strangeness was familiar.

This familiarity was discovered, not expected. I thought, 'Rousseau, Le Douanier, painted this forest – perhaps that's why I know it.' But no. What he painted had existed before him: a version of the ancient pastoral dream in which all is sweet ease and irresponsibility. It was a version dreamed in the cold and strenuous parts of Europe, a vision of the tropics as the sun's country untamed, the other side of life where people went innocently naked in forests like these and fruit fell into their hands. That was the dream that I was in.

It is to be seen not only in the forest but also in the pastoral glades of the little coastal plain where fawn cattle are tethered in the patterned shade of coconut palms – great groves of palms tilting gracefully this way and that, their fruit lying in the grass beneath. And you see it in the village gardens with their dark-leaved fruit trees. 'You know, don't you,' I was told, 'that you can always pick a fruit if you are thirsty? No one here will mind if you pick a fruit from his tree.' It was El Dorado. The mountains of diamonds and cities of gold had soon faded away, but the abundance, beauty and silence of the landscape which, inseminated by greed, gave birth to those illusions were still here. I felt that now, in these happy post-war years, I had come home to a dream and I wanted to go on living in it.

Many Europeans and North Americans were feeling this, and some of them had enough money to act on the feeling. They bought land and they built a house. I knew one very lovely house where friends of mine lived in elegant and knowledgeable enjoyment of the island. They had learnt its history and studied its flora and fauna; they followed its politics; they participated in local life. They lived a long way from the town, so their neighbours appreciated their running a fishing boat and selling their catch, breeding pigs and selling their meat, both very cheaply. They gave sick people lifts to hospital and helped when the authorities had to be approached about a pension or the sale of land. They invited young people to their house for 'talk-ins', knowing how frustrated they could be in a society too small to offer much intellectual exercise. They did a great deal that is useful and kind, besides enjoying themselves greatly, with so much discrimination and charm that it almost seemed their *raison d'être*. They seemed to have mastered the art of coming home to a dream without being lost to waking life. But although I liked and admired them, they made me feel uneasy.

I went to another house about a mile away from theirs: one of half a dozen strung out along a mountain road, built of wood and corrugated iron, propped on groggy-looking stilts and appearing to European eyes more like a henhouse or a garden shed than a dwelling place. I was seeing a man about some pillowcases – he was the only person left who still practised the craft of painting on fabric, which used to be quite common in Tobago. My friends knew about this craft and liked to put work in the way of its last practitioner. His house had two small rooms and a porch on which stood the oil stove for cooking. The room I saw was unpainted, carefully swept but looking dirty because all its brown-grey surfaces were so worn that they could not look otherwise. It contained a table, one chair (there was another on the porch), a shelf nailed to the wall with an enamel basin and a few cups and plates on it, a calendar, and a cotton curtain on a wire across the window, so faded that its colours were unidentifiable. The man was not out of work – he could paint pillowcases only at weekends – so he was not unusually unlucky, and his family was small. It was common to see many children playing around or under just such a house, and until then I had not wondered how they all fitted in at night and how they looked so neat and clean on their long walks to and from school. At school-out time the roads swarmed with beautiful children trooping home, and only a few of them *looked* as though they lived in houses without drainage, where water had to be fetched from a standpipe down the road. The painter was perhaps unusual in that his family was all afflicted in some way – he had a diseased eye, his wife was dropsical and his son had impetigo – but after I had visited him and had started to look more attentively at the villages I passed through, I began to suspect that the impression of healthiness given by the people on this island as a whole might be superficial.

It would be hard to starve to death (though easy enough to be malnourished) in the middle of so much abundance, in such a kind climate. If you wanted to go naked you could do so without discomfort, so having no shoes and only a ragged shirt wouldn't kill you either. But it was the very richness of what surrounded them that made the houses' poverty so shocking, as though you split a glossy fruit to find only a little wormy dust. I met Europeans who had come to run businesses in Tobago who said of the people in the villages, 'They never do more than they absolutely *have* to' – and I heard black people say it, too: black people who had escaped. The closer you looked, the more you wondered that so many did escape, because simply becoming accustomed to a life so reduced, which a person naturally has to do if it's the only life on offer, would shrink his mind and dry up his energy. Inertia was inevitable and simple-mindedness unsurprising. Only the truly exceptional individual can rise above being bone-poor in a tiny and remote society.

These people were here, in this condition, because their ancestors were enslaved by ours in order to keep the beautiful European dream going when it turned out that the only gold Tobago would provide would come from working the land: a let-down compared with conquering mythical cities, but not too bad if you could put enough two-legged livestock to work at no cost. When this stopped paying we tinkered about with other methods, and when they stopped paying we pulled out, congratulating ourselves on granting independence to what we left behind. Which, seen as an organized society, was the empty shell of European greed from which the omnivorous mollusc that had determined its shape had withdrawn; and seen humanly was a collection of people who had to decide what kind of society to become, given that they lived in very small places on the edge of the world, with few resources.

One method of survival had been to allow the white organism back on terms which suited it better than overt possession. It was the easiest method, bringing in quick money and avoiding an alarming collapse of the shell – the form of society to which everyone had become accustomed. It has been followed throughout the Caribbean except in Cuba. Oil, bauxite, sugar, bananas, citrus fruit, pitch, copra: they can all make money for someone, so it wasn't a question of coaxing the old mollusc back. Keeping him out – that would have been the problem (and has been, in Cuba).

Tobago is governed by its larger sister island, Trinidad, and had little say in the decision to exploit almost the only asset it possesses: its beauty. What other decision could have been made? But it is humiliating to have one's role decided for one, and worse when one can't afford to play it. No doubt Tobagonians would have been delighted to build their own resort hotels and make as much money as possible from their visitors, but they could operate on only the smallest scale. If a lot of tourists were to be tempted in, others had to finance the industry – so in came the companies from Britain, America and Canada, in negotiation with Port of Spain, the distant capital. They were making big investments, and when a development company makes a big investment it is because it confidently expects that it – it, and no one else – will make a big profit. It will grant, of course, that the profit must be taxed by the country in which it is operating, but it would take it ill if the tax approximated to what it would have to pay at home.

I happened to meet people working for such companies right at the start of my visit to Tobago, and it was apparent that for them the charm of a Caribbean island lay largely in its being so manageable. Their talk was all of the frustration – or the comedy – of inefficiency; but it is worth being frustrated almost to ulcer point when you can persuade a government that you are doing it a favour by operating in its territory, and can pay its people very modestly for their labour while getting credit for employing them at all. It is precisely the inefficiency which is valued. A people who operated as you operate, and expected from life what you expect, would be far more tiresome to deal with.

'The level of education,' I was told, 'is pathetic. One isn't supposed to say such things nowadays – ha, ha – but the best most of them can do is learn like parrots.' (That was one of the remarks which made me marvel at the lack of self-consciousness: how could he not realize that he was sounding just like a caricature of himself?) The level of education *was* low. You only had to talk to a few teachers to see it, either from the criticism of the system provided by the intelligent, or from the examples of what it produced provided by the dull. What shocked was the underlying (and probably unconscious) gloating: the unsaid, 'And long may it stay that way.'

Local people, even if liked, were spoken of with condescension. If a European described a local as able, he sounded as though he were trying to convince me of something surprising; if he said someone was 'a friend' there was a fractional pause in which I was supposed to note his broad-mindedness. The usual tone was knowing and jocular: they were 'priceless', these people, and some story would follow about bribery at high level or comic ineptitude at low. The 'pricelessness' of servants was a particularly popular subject: being 'priceless' was part of the servant's role (and it was not only the masters who knew it). All of them said how much they loved the place and its inhabitants. The secret of their knowing jocularity was that they loved it all because they felt themselves to be on top of it.

My friends in the lovely house didn't want to be on top of it. They were making no money out of it – were in fact contributing something to it and were eager to contribute more. What made me feel uneasy about their situation was what made me feel uneasy about my own. They lived in this place, and I was visiting it, because it was so enjoyable . . . and an element in our enjoyment would have been missing if everyone there had been having the same kind of good time as we were having. It was not just the simple matter of having more servants than you could have had at home: it came from being surrounded by people who reflected a flattering light on you. In such a society a sophisticated European knows more, and knows it better, than almost all his neighbours; whether he wants to be better equipped or not, in many ways he is. Part of the lingering dream of the sweet and easy life is being among sweet and simple people on whom you would in some way be able to look down, were you not *too kind and understanding to do so*. These people furnish your dream.

And while they do so – this is something you don't always notice, although you certainly should – you are furnishing theirs. Your money, your mobility, your education, your house, your clothes, your food, your books: they are dreaming of all this and they want to live in that dream more passionately, and with far better reason, than you want to live in yours.

I know from experience that this can't help being a corrupting relationship. Having been assured by a travel agent that the only hotels in the Caribbean were the expensive places designed for tourists, and having been offered a free stay in one of them by the company, which apparently believed that the words 'publisher' and 'publicity' are more closely related than they are, I had started my visit to Tobago in such an establishment. It was well-run and very comfortable, and I couldn't stand it. There may have been – probably were – people staying there who hired cars and drove about to see more of Tobago than I ever did, but if so I failed to see them. Rich old Americans wanting to enjoy familiar comforts in the sun, settling snugly into an ambience designed specifically for them – that was what I saw, and I decided at once that two days of polite acceptance of the hotel's hospitality must be endured, after which I must find somewhere else.

And on the second day I visited the public beach and was greeted by Mr Peters, who ran it. The beach had been provided for 'the people' as a sop after other and finer beaches had been leased to developers, but there were still miles of lovely shoreline from which anyone could swim, and the people would have preferred the money to be spent on roads, or a school, so Mr Peters and his staff had little to do, and a visitor had to be celebrated with a drink. When he asked where I was staying I told him, adding that I didn't much like it and found it hard to believe that no other kind of hotel could be found. 'Surely,' I said, 'there must be places where ordinary people stay?' There was a moment's hesitation while Mr Peters avoided exchanging a glance with his lieutenant and I remembered being told in Port of Spain that 'ordinary' in local usage meant 'niggery'; but they kindly decided to accept the word in my sense and said that of course there were. Mr Peters could take me to one then and there if I wished.

I could not have found a pleasanter little hotel – a small old estate house adapted and run by a retired schoolmaster and his wife, lifelong friends of Mr Peters, who would have been friendly to any guest and were specially so to me, because I was their very first (I was even shown the inside of the oven – spotless! – in the kitchen). And Mr Peters told them that I was 'all right'. I don't assume this; I heard him say it. He came by for drinks every evening, bringing friends to entertain me – he was a modest old man and thought himself dull company. We often talked politics (almost as inevitable in the Caribbean as in Ireland) and once or twice someone would pause and look embarrassed after being carried away into an anti-white remark. 'Don't worry,' Mr Peters would then say with proprietorial satisfaction. 'She's all right, you can say what you want to her,' and there would be a little stir of approval. It was not unmixed. There were undercurrents of suspicion (or at least, 'Let's wait and see') and embarrassment. But because they were friendly people and the smallness of the community made any stranger interesting, they let approval prevail – and it was flattering.

I could not resist enjoying it. One evening Mr Peters recalled my asking for a hotel where 'ordinary' people stayed, and we all laughed. They knew I hadn't particularly meant 'black', but that's what it had amounted to and I hadn't minded, so I was 'all right' and it could become a joke. And I, alas, felt pleased with myself. These people appeared to overvalue me, and I was enjoying it. In other words, I was getting pleasure as a result of other people's degradation: for what is it but degradation when black people have been conditioned to see it as something of an event when a white person accepts their company? And I think it was this kind of dubious pleasure that the island offered as a subtle 'extra' to my friends in their beautiful house.

The people I was with, who were also enjoying our evenings together, were just as capable as I was of recognizing its ambiguity, just as likely to feel uneasy at the little extra kick we were all getting out of each other's company because our skins were different colours and we were acting as though they were not. Absurd as it was that we should even notice it, history had dictated that we did. And if they recoiled from this fact they would have a great deal more reason to do so violently than I would.

I don't say that one shouldn't visit Caribbean countries because of this legacy, or that my friends should not have built a house there. If a dependent island becomes independent it has to learn to let the international bloodstream run through it, and the only way individuals can become sane about race is by plodding stubbornly on through the insanities. Many of them can be left behind, even within the span of one individual's experience, so something is gained: in spite of the undercurrents, encounters like those between me and Mr Peters and his friends are better than none. But I do say that the white visitor to the Caribbean should remember that the dream he is pursuing is remote from reality, and that reality was poisoned by his own ancestors and is still being poisoned by his brothers.

At the tail end of all colonial situations there are white people protesting that they didn't deserve to have stones thrown at them by black men, or their houses burnt down, because they never took a penny from the place and devoted years to serving it – and often they are not lying. But even when they are not, their lament reflects their illusions rather than the injustice of the event. The black people who gathered on Tobago's beaches to shout 'Get out Whitey!', and marched into hotels where they tore up visitors' books and broke ashtrays (they were by nature a mild and law-abiding lot who didn't want to hurt anybody) may conceivably, one day, burn down houses such as that of my friends. If that is all they do – and it may well be all, since there are few signs of constructive political thinking in Caribbean opposition politics – they will contribute nothing to their own welfare, but they will at least be expressing a more acute awareness of the truth than the people who built the houses. They will be saying that even if they cannot alter the economic structure which condemns them to exploitation, they will no longer stand being used as live furniture in someone else's beautiful dream.

Alive, Alive Oh!

In my early forties I thought of myself as a rational woman, but while I could sleep alone in an empty house for night after night without worrying, there were other nights when my nerves twitched like a rabbit's at the least sound, regardless of what I had been reading or talking about. On the many good nights and the few bad the chances of a burglar breaking in were exactly the same: the difference was within myself and signified nothing which I could identify. And I had always been like that over the possibility of pregnancy.

For several months it would not occur to me to worry, but then I would be convinced, perhaps as much as a fortnight before the month's end, that this time it had happened. The anxiety seemed in itself an indication: why this sudden fret if there were no reason? I would start working out how to find the money for an abortion, or whether I was capable of bringing up a child single-handed, and when the anxiety proved groundless I would feel foolish as well as relieved.

This last month had been an easy-minded one. I happened, for once, to know the date on which, in this sense, it should end, having filled an idle moment by marking little crosses in my diary some way ahead; but although I was often a few days early and never late, I was so far from worrying that I hardly noticed when the day came and went. Six more days passed before I said to myself: 'Hadn't you better start acknowledging this? The curse is six days overdue and your breasts are hurting.'

Rational? How did I square that with the fact that, in spite of the fluctuations in anxiety, I had taken no precautions against pregnancy for almost two years? From time to time, at the end of an anxious month, I had thought of it: 'If I'm let off this time I'll never be such a fool again.' But I never did anything about it. 'Not today,' 'Not this week,' 'Another time,' or even, 'What's the point? I'll only put the damned things in a drawer and forget to use them.' The mere thought of it seemed too tedious to bear. Although I had twice become pregnant in the past, that was now such a long time ago, and surely I had reached an age when it was less likely? After all, month after month had gone by to confirm my optimism.

If anyone had said to me, 'There can be only one reason for an unmarried woman in her early forties to ignore good sense so stubbornly: she does it not from an optimistic belief that she will not conceive, but because of an exactly opposite subconscious optimism: deep inside herself she wants a child,' I would have answered, 'Of course she does. I do know that, really. I suppose I must have been choosing to ignore it.' But although I had not been able to prevent my subconscious from undermining my reason, I saw nothing against putting it in its place. I had overruled it twice before and had felt no ill effects. 'All right, so you want a baby. Who doesn't? But as things are you can't have one – I'm sorry but there it is, too bad for you.' Neither time had it put up any fight. It had accepted its frustration placidly – and placidly it had resumed its scheming.

I had once met a man who had been persuaded to consult an analyst about, of all things, his constipation. He had found the experience interesting and beneficial, and summed it up in words that delighted me: 'It's fascinating to learn what an old juggins one's subconscious is.' That was what I now felt: what an old juggins! What a touching and in some ways admirable old juggins! I saw my subconscious plodding along, pigheaded, single-minded, an old tortoise lumbering through undergrowth, heaving itself over fallen branches, subsiding into holes full of dead leaves. Sometimes, no doubt, the obstacles had been almost too much for him and he had lain, panting slightly, staring up at the sky and blinking in apparent bewilderment, but then a blunt foreleg would begin to grope again, his toes would scratch for purchase and on he would go. The question was this: did I say, 'Impressive though such persistence is, he is still a juggins,' or did I say, 'Juggins he may be, but such persistence is impressive'? Did I, in other words, slap my subconscious down again by finding the necessary cash and the obliging doctor from the past (if he was still taking such risks), or did I capitulate and have this child?

The reasons against it were these: I was unmarried, forty-three years old and had no private income. I could live comfortably on what I earned, with nothing to spare. I would like to preserve these conditions.

The reasons for it were these: if I did not have a child now I would never have one, and I loved Barry, its father.

Barry was married – well married, to an admirable woman who had done him no wrong and to whom he owed much. He had begun an affair simply because he had been married for seven years, was no longer romantically in love with his wife, and was polygamous by nature. He had come to take the affair seriously because we suited each other in every way, one of our strongest bonds being that neither of us was possessive. He might have been described as sitting pretty, married to a good, dependable wife, without whom he could not imagine himself, and in love with a good, dependable mistress to whom he could turn whenever he wished. But it was more complex than that. I was nine years older than he, which, together with my nature, had given me a certain authority over the situation. He saw me as having *chosen* this form of relationship rather than having been persuaded or manoeuvred into it, and he was right: there was no reason why he should develop a sense of responsibility towards me except in our own terms of honesty and tenderness. It was a perfect situation for him, since he had no money and was trying to live by writing; but the fact that one partner is well suited does not necessarily mean that the other is ill used. I myself might have condemned some other woman's lover in a similar situation, but I knew him and myself too well to condemn him. He was what he was: the person with whom, *being as he was*, I was most at home. What, then, would be the point of wishing him otherwise?

And could I make him otherwise, if I wanted to? No. And I didn't mind that, because I was perfectly willing to accept that we, as we both were, were each other's unexpected bonus from life. It was this that had established so much ease and sweetness between us. If, when I told him I was pregnant, he were to offer to leave his wife and come to me, I would be quite as anxious as I would be happy. I would not, whatever I decided, try to make him do that. Perhaps this was cowardice – a fear of actually having to face a lack of success which I thought I could envisage with equanimity. Or perhaps it was vanity – a desire to go on representing freedom, pleasure, stimulation, all the joys of love rather than its burdens. Or perhaps it was really what I would like it to be: the kind of respect for another person's being that I would wish to have paid to my own. But there was no doubt that, if I was pregnant, life would be a great deal easier if my lover and my love were otherwise than they were.

So it would be sensible to have an abortion. In my experience it was not a profoundly disagreeable thing to have. The worst part of the actual operation, performed under a local anaesthetic, in the circumstances prevailing at the time when I first experienced it, was the grotesque position into which one had been trussed on the table. I had found that I could see a tiny but clear reflection of myself in the globe of the lampshade above me, and at that I almost lost grip but screwed my eyes shut instead. There was this humiliating ugliness, and there were sounds, and for a few moments there was a dim sensation of pain. If the doctor was businesslike and kind, treating one (as mine had done) like an ordinary patient, there was no sinister or shaming atmosphere to contend with. One was simply having a quick little operation for a sensible reason ... So it was odd that I should start to shiver slightly as I thought about it. No, I did not feel that a murder is committed during that operation. I would go so far as to say that I was sure it was not: no separate existence, at that stage, was being ended, any more than when a sperm was prevented from meeting an egg. But that old juggins, the pin-headed, pig-headed tortoise behind my reason: he was tough, he was good at recovering from setbacks, but at the prospect of yet another of them he was showing signs of turning into a porcupine. He wanted me to have this child.

~

Having acknowledged the situation, I found myself no nearer a decision, only slightly more aware of reluctance towards either course. It was still early. I could have an abortion, if I so decided, at any time within the next three months. So the best thing to do seemed to me to be nothing: go blank, drift for a week or so, think about it as little as possible and see what happened. Perhaps I would wake up one morning knowing what I wanted to do.

The next two weeks dragged. I managed to keep my mind on other things for much of the time, but the fact of pregnancy was always there, lying in wait for any unoccupied moment. It seemed common sense not to begin worrying again at least until I had missed my second period, but long before that date came I felt that my condition had endured for months. Each morning, when I awoke, I would lie still for a minute or two trying to overhear my state of mind, but all I picked up was irritation and depression at being in this quandary. About ten days after the start of my 'truce' I spent a weekend in the country with my mother, and the depression increased: supposing I had the child, how appalling the family explanations would be, how impossible it was to imagine the degree of consternation such a decision would raise in my mother and the rest of the family. In the train on the way back to London I looked up from my book and bumped, as usual, into, 'What am I going to do?' 'Oh God,' I thought, 'I do wish *it would all go away*.'

'Well,' I thought next morning, 'if that's the best I can do I suppose I had better *make* it go away: get the money in, anyway.' There was a sum waiting for me in New York, where I had planned soon to spend a holiday. If I called in half of that, would there be enough left for the holiday? Probably not. Resentment and disappointment were added to the depression, but I called my agent with a story of unexpected bills as a result of moving house, and he cabled me the money at once. That done, I had only to call the doctor – his number, on a grubby scrap of paper, discreetly minus his name, still lurked at the back of a drawer in my dressing table after all those years. 'I'll do it soon,' I thought. 'Next week, perhaps. I've got the money and that's the main thing.' I spent a couple of days in a rage at missing my first chance to visit New York, and another couple arguing that I needn't miss it after all: if I spent only three weeks there instead of four, and lived very cheaply, I could manage. If that were so, I was not only being sensible, I was not going to suffer for it, so there was nothing to be depressed about any more.

It was on the fifth morning after the arrival of the money – a morning in April – that I awoke congratulating myself on living in my new flat and opening my eyes in my new bedroom. It was the top floor of a house which might almost be in the country – the last house in a short street which projected like a little promontory into a park. All the windows looked onto trees and grass, and my bedroom window had gardens as well, the long range of gardens behind the houses of the street at right angles to mine. Cherry and pear trees were in flower, and a fine magnolia; daffodils and narcissi twinkled in the grass. Soon the lilacs would be out, and the hawthorns, and the irises – it was a galloping spring after a mild winter. The sun shone through my bedroom window, and the birds were singing so loudly that they had woken me before my alarm clock went off: each garden seemed to have its own blackbird. I got out of bed to lean out of the window and sniff the green smells, and found myself saying: 'What a morning for birds and bees and buds and babies.'

This sentence was still humming in my mind as I walked to the bus stop, past the walls of more gardens, not high enough to conceal the trees and shrubs behind them. During the previous winter, before moving into the flat, I had thought as I walked this way: 'This will soon be my part of London – I shall see that pear, that crab-apple tree in flower, and then heavy with dusty summer green, and then with hard little London fruit on their branches – they will be familiar landmarks.' And there they were, going into their spring performance with abandon against a brilliant blue sky, part of my daily walk to the bus. 'It is a lovely place to live,' I thought. 'I suppose I *am* going to have this baby after all.'

I was late, I had to run for a bus, those words evaporated and no thought of my predicament disturbed my morning's work. Then my business partner came into my room, to spring on me a discussion of long-term plans for the firm. Someone might be persuaded to join us and if he did shares would have to be reallocated, certain changes of status would have to be made. 'It concerns you, too,' he said, 'so you must think it over.' I had a slight sensation of breathlessness and could feel my face flushing, but I made no decision to say what in fact I did say: 'I don't know that it *will* concern me. I may not be here then. I'm going to have a baby.' And inside my head I was saying: 'At last! The cat has jumped at last.' I was also saying: 'Oh lord, now I've done it!' – but the dismay was a laughing dismay, not a horrified one.

Perhaps my mood would not have held if my news had been received differently. As it was, my partner, a very old friend, said: 'You mean you're pregnant *now*?'

'Yes.'

'Have you seen a doctor?'

'Not yet... of course it may be a mistake, but I'm sure it's not.'

'Well, then, are you mad?' he said, sitting down on the radiator, frowning. 'How do you think you're going to support the child if you don't stay on here?'

'Oh, somehow – people do manage. And I thought it might be a bit embarrassing in the office...'

'Good God! If anyone's embarrassed they can bloody well get out!'

Then, dropping his poker face, he asked if I had really thought he would expect me to leave, and I answered that of course I hadn't, but it had seemed that it would be such an imposition... each of us slightly awkward at being pitched so suddenly into full awareness of our long and usually taken-for-granted affection for each other, and me the more so for having to produce thoughts which I had not yet formed about the practical side of this pregnancy. Then he kissed me and said that he was happy for me, and I was left grinning across my desk like the Cheshire cat, established in my full glory as an Expectant Unmarried Mother.

After that I was happy. I was quite often frightened too, but on a superficial level compared with the happiness. The birth would be easy. I could take as much time off as I needed, drawing my salary all the while, and for so long as I could stay at home all would be simple. The house in which I had my flat was owned by a cousin of mine who herself lived in the rest of it, and who from the moment I told her of the pregnancy was eager to help. Neither of us had much money – I myself had to let one of the rooms in my flat to help pay its modest rent – so I was anxious not to become a financial burden on my cousin, but it was reassuring to know that if the worst came to the worst I would never be chased for the rent. But I could not take advantage of that reassurance for more than a short time, and didn't want to do even that. And in addition to my usual living expenses I would have to pay for someone to care for the child while I was working, and for its food and clothes, and for its education – no, it would go to a state school, of course, there was a good one nearby – but for its bicycle and its roller skates and its holidays by the sea ... Year after year of financial strain stretched ahead. Financial strain and, to start with at any rate, physical exhaustion: office all day, child for every other minute – would I ever again be free to write? Not for years, anyway.

And no less frightening was the thought of the gap in the child's life where a father ought to be. Material considerations could be smothered by 'I'll manage somehow – people do'; of course I would manage when I had to. But the argument advanced by my more sober-minded friends, and by my own mind as well, that one has no right to wish this lopsided upbringing on any child – that was less easy. Surely only an exceptional woman could reasonably expect to steer her child comfortably through the shoals of illegitimacy, and could I make any claim to be exceptional? To this question I found I could make no answer. I could only say: 'Whatever happens, whatever the child itself may one day say (and there probably *will* come a time when it will say, "I never asked to be born"), I believe that it will prefer to exist rather than not.' But the real answer was not in those words, nor in any others that I might think up. It was simply in the rock-like certainty that the cat had jumped; that now, come what may and whatever anyone said, it was beyond me to consider an abortion. When I tried to force myself to think about it, I felt as though something physical happened in my skull, as though an actual shutter came down between the front part of my brain, just behind my eyes, where the thought began, and the back of my brain, where it would have to go if it were to be developed.

The biggest immediate worry was how to tell my mother, whose outlook would make it very hard for her to accept such news. I veered between a desire to get the worst over by writing at once, and a longing to put it off for ever. Barry advised me to put it off for a month or so, just in case something went wrong, and finally I agreed, throwing a sop to my itch to get it over by writing in advance the letter I would send later, choosing a time just before one of my visits home so that my mother could get over the worst of the shock before we discussed it. I enjoyed writing that letter: putting into words how much I wanted a child and how determined to have this one I had now become. I found my letter so convincing that I couldn't believe my mother would not agree.

The longing to tell everyone else was strong. I scolded myself, arguing that when I began to bulge would be soon enough; people *did* have miscarriages, and no discreet woman would announce a pregnancy before the fourth month. But with every day discretion became less important, jubilation grew stronger, and I had soon told everyone with whom I was intimate and some with whom I was not. Almost all my friends appeared to be delighted for me, and their support gave me great pleasure. Sometimes they said I was brave, and I enjoyed that too, in spite of knowing that courage did not come into it; it was just that the tortoise had won. The interest and sympathy that seemed to surround me was like a good wine added to a delicious dinner.

Barry was, in a detached way, pleased. The pregnancy made no difference to the form of our relationship, but it did deepen it: his tenderness and attention were a comfort and a pleasure. I wondered, sometimes, what would happen about *that* once the child was born: would an 'uncle' in its life instead of a father be a good thing or a bad one? We would have to see. I knew that if it proved a bad thing I would have to lose Barry – would lose him without hesitation however great the pain – but for the present having him there was a large, warm part of the happiness which carried the anxieties like driftwood on its broad tide.

I felt gloriously well, hungry, lively and pretty, without a single qualm of sickness and with only a shadow of extra fatigue at the end of a long day, from time to time. 'Well, *you* seem to be all right,' they said to me at the hospital clinic which I began to attend. During the long waits at this clinic I watched the other women and thought that none of them looked so well or so pleased as I did. At my first visit I kept quiet, half anxious and half amused by doubts as to how my spinsterhood would be treated by the nurses and doctors, but once I discovered that it was taken not only calmly but with extra kindness, I relaxed. One of the other expectant mothers, very young, was like myself in having suffered nothing in the way of sickness or discomfort, and the two of us made an almost guilty smug corner together. I contrived to read details about myself over the shoulder of a nurse who was filling in a form about me, and glowed with ridiculous pride at all the 'satisfactories' and at 'nipples: good'.

However simple and quick the examination itself, the clinic proved always to take between two and three hours, so I arranged to see my own doctor regularly instead. As I left the clinic for the last time I happened to be thinking – worrying – about the problem of the child's care while I was at the office, when a man leant out of the cab of a passing truck and shouted at me: 'That's right, love – keep smiling!' Worrying I may have been, but I was also grinning all over my face.

Those weeks of April and May were the only ones in my life when spring was wholly, fully beautiful. All other springs carried with them regret at their passing. If I thought, 'Today the white double cherries are at their most perfect,' it summoned up the simultaneous awareness: 'Tomorrow the edges of their petals will begin to turn brown.' This time a particularly ebullient, sun-drenched spring simply *existed* for me. It was as though, instead of being a stationary object past which a current was flowing, I was flowing with it, in it, at the same rate. It was a happiness new to me, but it felt very ancient, and complete.

One Saturday, soon after my last clinic, Barry came to see me at lunchtime. I had got up early and done a big shop, but not a heavy one, because a short time before I became pregnant I had bought a basket on wheels (was it coincidence that several of my purchases just before the condition were of things suited to it: that basket, the slacks which were rather too loose round the waist, with the matching loose top?). I left the basket at the bottom of the stairs for him to bring up, because, strong and well though I felt, I was taking no foolish risks. We ate a good lunch, both of us cheerful and relaxed. After it he was telling me a funny story when I interrupted with, 'Wait a minute, I must go to the loo – tell me when I get back,' and hurried out to have a pee, wanting to get back quickly for the end of the story. When I saw blood on the toilet paper my mind went, for a moment, quite literally blank.

So I got up and went slowly back into the sitting room, thinking, 'To press my fingers against my cheek like this must look absurdly overdramatic.'

'I'm bleeding,' I said in a small voice.

He scrambled up from the floor, where he'd been lying, and said, 'What do you mean? Come and sit down. How badly?'

'Only a very little,' I said, and began to tremble.

He took me by the shoulders and pulled me against him, saying quieting things, saying, 'It's all right, we'll ring the doctor, it's probably nothing,' and although I didn't know I was going to start crying, I felt myself doing it. I had not yet been able to tell what I was feeling, but suddenly I was having to control myself hard in order not to scream. 'The important thing,' he said, 'is to find out.' He went to fetch the telephone directory and said: 'Come on, now, ring the doctor.'

The telephone was near my chair, so I didn't have to move, which I felt was important. The doctor was off duty for the weekend, but a stand-in answered. Any pain? No. How much bleeding? I explained how little. Then there was nothing to be done but to go to bed at once and stay there for forty-eight hours. 'Does this necessarily mean a miscarriage?' I asked. No, certainly not. How would I know if it turned into one? It would seem like an exceptionally heavy period, with the passing of clots. If that happened I must telephone again, but otherwise just stay lying down.

Barry ran out to buy me sanitary towels. During the few minutes I was alone I found myself crying again, flopped over the arm of my chair, tears streaming down my face, saying over and over again in a sort of whispered scream, 'I don't *want* to have a miscarriage, I don't *want* to have a miscarriage.' I knew it was a silly thing to be doing, and when my cousin, alerted by Barry, came, I was relieved to find that I could pull myself together, sit up and talk.

They put me to bed, and we talked about other women we knew of who had bled during pregnancy with no ill effect, and I soon became calm. During the next two days the bleeding became even less, but it did not quite stop, and over the phone my doctor repeated his colleague's words: no one could do anything, it was not necessarily going to be a miscarriage, I would know all right if it became one, and I must stay in bed until it stopped. I was comfortable in my pretty bedroom, reading Jane Austen almost non-stop for her calming quality (I reread the whole of *Mansfield Park*, *Northanger Abbey*, *Persuasion* and *The Watsons* in four days), listening to the radio and doing a little office work. By the fourth day my chief anxiety had become not the possibility of a miscarriage, but the fear that this slight bleeding might tie me to my bed not for days but for weeks. A bedridden pregnancy would be bad enough for anyone, but for me, entirely dependent as I was on friends who all had jobs or families ... How could they possibly go on doing as much as they were doing now for much longer?

I was lucky in one way: anxiety, fear and certain kinds of misery always had an almost anaesthetic effect on me, making my mind and feelings sluggish. Under such stresses I shrank into the moment, just doing the next thing to be done, and sleeping a lot. So those four days passed in a state of suspended emotion rather than in unhappiness – suspended emotion stabbed every now and then with irritation at the absurdity of having to fear disaster when I was feeling as well as ever. It was ridiculous!

During the night of the fourth day I came slowly out of sleep at three in the morning to a vague feeling that something was amiss. It took me a minute or two of sleepy wondering before I identified it more exactly. Not since I was a girl had I suffered any pain during my period – I had almost forgotten what kind of pain it was – but now . . . yes. In a dim, shadowy way it was that old pain that was ebbing and flowing in my belly. When it ebbed I thought, 'Quick, go to sleep again, you were imagining it.' But it came back, its fluctuations confirming its nature. More anaesthetized than ever, barely awake, I got up, fetched a bucket from the kitchen and a newspaper to fold and use as a lid, and a big towel from the linen cupboard. I arranged all this beside my bed and went to sleep again.

When I woke an hour and a half later it was because blood was trickling over my thigh. 'This is it': dull resentment was what I felt. I hitched myself out of bed and over the bucket – and woke with a cold shock at the thudding gush, the sensation that a cork had blown. 'Oh God, oh God,' I thought, 'I didn't know it would be like this.' Blood ran fast for about half a minute, then dwindled to a trickle. Swaddling myself in the towel, I lay back on the bed, telling myself that no doubt it had to be fairly gruesome to start with.

After that the warning trickle came every ten or fifteen minutes, out over the bucket I went, terrified that I might overturn it with a clumsy gesture as I removed and restored the newspaper lid. The gush was never as violent as the first one, but each time it was violent and it did not diminish. I tried not to see the dark, clotted contents of the bucket – it was only when I saw it that I almost began to cry. There was a peppery smell of blood, but if I turned my head in a certain way I could catch a whiff of fresh air from the window, which lessened it. It was already light when I woke the second time, and soon after that the first blackbird began to sing. I lay still between the crises, watching the sun's first rays coming into the room and trying to make out how many blackbirds were singing behind the one in our own garden.

My cousin would be coming up to give me breakfast. She usually came at eight – but it might be later. 'If she doesn't come till late . . .' I thought, and became tearful. Then I decided to wait until seven-thirty, by which time the bleeding would surely be diminished, and telephone her – with the towel between my legs I would be able to get to the sitting room, where the phone was. The thought of telephoning the doctor myself was too much, because if his number were engaged or he were out I couldn't bear it; my cousin must do it. Time was going very fast, I noticed, looking at the alarm clock on the corner of my chest of drawers. That was something, anyway.

I had come out in a heavy sweat after the first flow, but it was not until about six-thirty that it happened again. Then sweat streamed off me and I was icy cold, and – worse – I began to feel sick. The thought of having to complicate the horror by vomiting into that dreadful bucket put me in a panic, so when the sweating was over and the nausea had died away, immediately after another violent flow, I knew I must get to the telephone now. I huddled the towel between my legs, stood up, took two steps towards the door, felt myself swaying, thought quite clearly, 'They are wrong when they say everything goes black; it's not going black, it's disappearing. I must fall onto the bed.' Which I did.

The next hour was vague, but I managed to follow my routine: bucket, paper back, flat on bed, wrap dressing gown over belly. I began to feel much iller, with more sweating, more cold, more nausea. When I heard my lodger moving about in his room next door I knew I had to call him. He knew nothing of my pregnancy – thought I had been in bed with an upset stomach. We were so far from being intimate that even if I had thought of him I might have felt unable to call him. Now I tapped on the wall and called his name, but he didn't hear. A little more time passed, and I heard him in the passage outside my door and called again. This time he heard, and answered, and I told him to go downstairs and fetch my cousin. 'You mean now?' came his startled voice through the door. 'Yes, quickly.' Oh, that was wonderful, the sound of his feet hurrying away, and only a minute or two later my door opened and in came my cousin.

One look and she ran for the telephone without saying a word. She caught the doctor in his surgery, two minutes before he went out on a call. He arrived so soon that it seemed almost at once, looked into the bucket, felt my pulse, pulled down my eyelid and left the room quickly to call an ambulance and alert the hospital. I felt hurt that neither he nor my cousin had spoken to me, but now my cousin said could I drink a cup of tea and I felt it would be wonderful – but couldn't drink it when it appeared. The relief of not having to worry any more would have been exquisite, if it had not given me more time to realize how ill I was feeling. The ambulance men wrapped me in a beautiful big red blanket and said not to worry about bleeding all over it (so that's why ambulance blankets are usually red). The breath of fresh air as I was carried across the pavement made me feel splendidly alert after the dreadful dizziness of being carried downstairs, so I asked for a cigarette and they said it wasn't allowed in the ambulance but I could have one all the same, and to put the ash in the sick bowl. One puff, and I felt much worse than ever; my cousin had to wipe the sweat off my forehead with a paper handkerchief. There was a pattern by then: a slowly mounting pain, a gush of blood, the sweating and nausea following at once and getting worse every time, accompanied by a terrible feeling that was not identifiable as pain but simply as *illness*. It made me turn my head from side to side and moan, although it seemed wrong to moan without intolerable pain.

The men carried me into a cubicle in the casualty department, and I didn't want them to leave because they were so kind. As soon as I was there the nausea came again, worse than ever so that this time I vomited, and was comforted because one of the men held my head and said, 'Never mind, dear.' A nurse said brusquely, while I was vomiting (trying to catch me unawares, I supposed), 'Did you have an injection to bring this on?' My 'no' came out like a raucous scream, which made me feel apologetic, so I had to gasp laboriously, 'I wanted most terribly to have this baby.' The man holding my head put his other hand on my arm and gave it a great squeeze, and that was the only time anyone questioned me.

My head cleared a bit after I had been sick. I noticed that the nurse couldn't find my pulse, and that when the doctor who soon came was listening to my heart through his stethoscope, he raised his eyebrows a fraction and pursed his lips, and then turned to look at my face, not as one looks at a face to communicate, but with close attention. I also noticed that they could never hear my answers to their questions, although I thought I was speaking normally. 'They think I'm really bad,' I said to myself, but I didn't feel afraid. They would do whatever had to be done to make me better.

It went on being like that up on the ward, when they began to give me blood transfusions. My consciousness was limited to the narrow oblong of my body on the stretcher, trolley or bed, and to the people doing things to it. Within those limits it was sharp, except during the recurring waves of horribleness, but it did not extend to speculation. When a nurse, being kind, said, 'You may not have lost the baby – one can lose a great deal of blood and the baby can still be all right,' I knew that was nonsense but felt nothing about it. When a doctor said to someone, 'Call them and tell him he must hurry with that blood – say that he must run,' I saw that things had gone further than I supposed but did not wonder whether he would run fast enough. When, a little later, they were discussing an injection and the same doctor said, 'She's very near collapse,' I thought perfectly clearly, 'Near collapse, indeed! If what I'm in now isn't collapse, it must be their euphemism for dying.' It did, then, swim dimly through my mind that I ought to think or feel something about this, but I hadn't the strength to produce any more than: 'Oh, well, if I die, I die,' and that thought, once registered, did not set up any echoes. The things which were real were the sordidness of lying in a puddle of blood, and the oddness of not minding when they pushed needles into me.

I also wanted to impress the nurses and doctors. Not till afterwards did I understand that I had slipped back into childhood; that the total trust in these powerful people, and the wish to make them think, 'There's a good, clever girl,' belonged in the nursery. I wanted to ask them intelligent questions about what they were doing, and to make little jokes – provided I could do so in not more than four or five words, because more would be beyond me. It was annoying that they seemed not to hear my little mumblings, or else just said, 'Yes, dear,' looking at my face as they said it with that same odd, examining expression. I made a brief contact with one of the doctors when he told them to do something 'to stop me being agitated'. What I wanted to say was, 'Don't be silly, I can't wait for you to get me down to the theatre and start scraping,' but all that came out was a peevish, 'Not agitated!' to which he replied politely, 'I'm sorry, of course you're not.' The only words I spoke from a deeper level than these feeble attempts at exhibitionism were when someone who was manipulating the blood bottle asked me if I was beginning to feel sleepy. It was during a wave of badness, and I heard my own voice replying hoarsely: 'I'm feeling *very ill.*'

I had always dreaded the kind of anaesthetic one breathes, because of a bad experience when I was having my appendix out, but when I understood that they were about to give me that kind and began to attempt a protest, I suddenly realized that I didn't give a damn: let them hurry up, let them get that mask over my face and I would go with it willingly. This had been going on much, much too long and all I wanted was the end of it.

The operation must have been a quick one, under a light anaesthetic, because when I woke up to an awareness of hands manipulating me back into bed, I was confused only for an instant, and only as to whether this was happening before or after the operation. That question was answered at once by the feeling in my belly: it was calm, I was no longer bleeding. I tried to move my hand down to touch myself in confirmation, and a nurse caught it and held it still – I hadn't realized that there was still a transfusion needle taped into the back of it. Having moved, I began to vomit. I had a deep-seated neurotic queasiness about vomiting, a horror of it, and until that moment I would never have believed that I could have been sick while lying flat on my back with the bowl so awkwardly placed under my chin that the sick went into my hair, and been happy while doing it.

But that was what was happening. An amazing glow of relief and joy was flowing up from my healed belly.

'I AM ALIVE.'

It was enough.

It was everything. It was filling me to the brim with pure and absolute joy, a feeling more intense than any I had known before. And very soon after that I was wondering why they were bothering to set up a new bottle of plasma, because I could have told them that all I needed now was to rest.

~

So if I were pinned down to answer the question, 'What did you feel on losing your child?' the only honest reply would be, 'Nothing.' Nothing at all, while it was going on. What was happening was so bad – so nearly fatal – that it eclipsed its own significance. And during the four days I spent in hospital I felt very little: no more than a detached acknowledgement that it was sad. Hospital routine closed round me gently, isolating me in that odd, childish world where girls in their early twenties are the 'grown-ups', and the exciting events are visiting time and being allowed to get up and walk to the lavatory. When it was time to go home I was afraid that I would hate my bedroom, expecting to have a horror of the blackbird's song and perhaps of some little rusty stain on the blue carpet, but friends took me home to an accompaniment of flowers, delicacies and cheerful talk, and I saw that it was still a pleasant room, my flat still a lovely place to live.

There was even relief: I would not now have to tell my mother anything, and I would not have to worry about money any more than usual. I could spend some on clothes for my holiday as soon as I liked, and I saw that I would enjoy the clothes and the holiday. It was this that was strange and sad, and made me think so often of how happy I had been while I was expecting the child (not of how unhappy I was now, because I wasn't). This was what sometimes gave me a dull ache, like a stomach ache but not physical: that someone who didn't yet exist could have the power to create spring, and could then be gone, and that once he was gone (I had always thought of the child as a boy), he became, because he had never existed, so completely gone: that the only tears shed for him were those first, almost unconscious tears shed by my poor old tortoise of a subconscious rather than by me. 'I *don't want* to have a miscarriage.' Oh, no, no, no, I hadn't wanted it, it was the thing I *didn't want* with all my heart. Yet now it had happened, and I was the same as I had always been ... except that now I knew – although if I had died during the miscarriage I would hardly, because of my physical state, have noticed it – the truth was that I loved being alive so much that not having died was more important to me by far than losing the child: more important than *anything.*

This Bit Ought Not to be True

There is a peculiarly English middle-class technique for dealing with awkward facts, about which I know a good deal from personal experience: if something is disagreeable let's pretend it isn't there.

I loved my family and my family loved me, but quite early in my life I began to see that loving people didn't necessarily mean agreeing with them. My family all appeared to believe what we were taught to believe in church. By the age of fifteen I knew that I didn't. They all voted Conservative. I knew that when I was old enough I was going to vote Labour. They all took it for granted that girls remained chaste until they married. I – although for my first twenty years I fully expected to get married and be faithful to a beloved man for the rest of my days – was perfectly sure that as soon as I got a chance to start making love I would grab it. If they knew all this, particularly that last item, they would almost certainly feel that they ought to cast me out – and I did not want to be cast out, nor were they by nature caster-outers, so the obvious solution to the problem was for me to keep quiet about what I thought and felt, and when those thoughts and feelings became apparent, as some of them did when I stopped going to church and read a lot of left-wing books, for them to pretend not to notice or to treat what they had to notice as a joke.

In my youth I found this hypocrisy shaming. Surely I ought to have stood by my beliefs and argued in their favour, and my family would have ended by respecting me for it. That was probably true as far as religion and politics were concerned, but sex was another matter, probably because my attitude about that was the result not of reasoning, but of my physical nature. Although the way in which it was going to make me live did not shock me, I could see all too clearly why it might shock other people, which meant that I couldn't be quite sure that it was not in fact shocking: the ground under my feet, in this matter, was not quite firm. Things could be foreseen (and were in fact to occur) which my family would quite certainly find hard to stomach, so, shaming or not, silence was best.

With this conclusion they silently agreed, as became clear on the publication of my first book in the 1960s. Although I failed to understand this until the book was written, it had been a therapeutic exercise. I hadn't planned the book. Absurd though it sounds to say, 'It happened to me,' it really did. I was astonished when it began, and went on being surprised, paragraph by paragraph, as it continued, returning to it every evening when I got home from the office with the utmost eagerness but with no idea of what was coming next. All I knew was that I had got to get it right.

It was the story of having my heart broken: something I had long stopped thinking about but which had been weighing on me as a suppressed sense of failure for years, and there was no point in telling the story unless I could really get to the bottom of it. Which I did, and, sure enough, it changed my life, which was truly marvellous ... but what on earth would my mother think of this brutal (to her) publication of such a mass of what (to her) ought to remain guilty secrets? It was she who mattered. My father was dead by then, and what the rest of the family was likely to feel was not greatly important to me.

I decided that the best thing to do was let the book be published in the USA, where she knew nobody so needn't worry about 'What will the neighbours think?', and then present it to her as a published book so that she could see that it could be considered acceptable, telling her that if she really couldn't bear it I would not let it be published here. So I put it in the post to her, and waited. And waited. And waited. Days turned into weeks, and still nothing. And I found myself unable to put my hand to the telephone and ask her, 'Did you receive my book?' I knew how silly this was, but I just *could not do it.* I had known that her decision was important to me, but had no idea, until gripped by this extraordinary inhibition, of *how* important it was.

Then we were both invited to stay for a weekend with her oldest friend, my godmother, so I said to myself, 'I'll ask her when we are at Aunt Phoebe's.' But no, I couldn't. She was to stay the night with me in London before going home to Norfolk, so, 'I'll ask her on the drive to London.' But still I couldn't. We got to my flat and it became, 'I'll ask her after we've had supper . . .' and while I was in the kitchen cooking it, thank God, the phone rang and she called out, 'It's Andrew – he wants to talk to you.' Andrew was my brother, and what did he say? 'Di, Mum wants you not to publish that book but I've told her that's rubbish. It's a bloody good book.' My knees almost gave way under me with the relief of it. I turned to look at her. 'I know, darling,' she said. 'He thinks I oughtn't to ask you, so I suppose I shouldn't?' and I said, 'Yes, perhaps you really shouldn't.' And we spent the rest of the evening talking about what was in that book – two adult women, talking calmly and openly about it, while I rejoiced inwardly at this lovely opening up of our relationship . . . and from that evening on she never once said another word to me about the book or anything in it. I always sent her copies of reviews so that she could see that it had shocked no one, but never once did she refer to them. I knew now that she had always been aware of almost everything in it, but it and its contents no longer existed.

At first I thought this was ridiculous, and so it was: ridiculous and dishonest. Then I thought it was comic. And finally, as the years went by, I came to see it as a very successful way of dealing with a difficult problem. You have a daughter whom you love, she does something you wish very much she hadn't done, but you want to go on loving her in spite of it. All right, so let's forget about it, let's wipe it out. It works! My mother and I grew closer and closer. There are no memories that I value more than that of the almost flame of love which lit her eyes when she opened them and saw me bending over her deathbed.

The Decision

Few events in my life have been decided by me. How I was educated, where I have lived, why I am not married, how I have earned my living: all these crucial things happened to me rather than were made to happen by me. Of course an individual's nature determines to some extent what happens, but moments at which a person just says, 'I shall now do X,' and does it are rare – or so it has been in my life. Perhaps my decision to move into a home for old people is not quite the only one, but it is certainly the biggest.

This is not to say that outside events contributed nothing to it, because two of them did set the scene. The first was a visit to a friend, Rose Hacker, after I learned that she had made such a move. This shook me, because Rose, though well over ninety, was a lively and independent woman. Rose in an old people's home? It seemed unthinkable. I decided I must summon up the nerve to visit her: 'summon up the nerve' because the image in my mind of such homes was a grim one.

This one, behind a wall in Highgate, north London, was set in a large, well-kept garden surrounded by trees and appeared to be uninhabited. I realize now that most of the residents were in the library, where tea is served to those who don't prefer to have it in their rooms, and that the staff were having theirs in their office, but wandering about unsupervised felt a bit creepy. Finally I met another wanderer, a visitor, but familiar with the place, and was guided to Rose's room. I knocked on the door. Silence. So I opened it, and there was Rose, who must by then have been rising a hundred, having a nap in a splendid extending armchair.

She woke at once, unabashed, and no sooner had she greeted me warmly than she said: 'My dear, you must come and live here. It is the most wonderful place.' I had no intention of living in any such place, but I was so relieved at finding Rose so happy that I urged her to tell me more, and her glowing report must have lodged in my mind, ready to pop out if need arose.

The second person to set the scene was Nan Taylor, who I had known since our taxis pulled up nose to tail outside Lady Margaret Hall, the Oxford college at which we were both nervously arriving. Nan was three months younger than me, but she weathered less well. By the time she was eighty she became really frail, so a bad fall led to a broken hip and soon my dearest old friend was an immobilized and incontinent wreck. She could afford agency nurses, who came every morning and evening, and had an angelic Irish cleaner who did much for her, but friends too had to rally round, which they did gladly because they loved her. It did, however, become a burden, and after two years I for one was regretting her determination to die in her own home.

I visited her twice a week, which entailed frantic searches for a parking space and an anxious wait at her front door. She would give no one but her carers and her nearest neighbour a key, so was she slowly making her precarious way to the door, or had she fallen? Often it was the latter, so I would have to call the neighbour, praying someone was at home, or, if they weren't, the police (who responded quickly and kindly, though climbing through her sitting-room window was not easy). And once Nan was safely back in her chair and tea had been made and administered, it became increasingly hard to penetrate her indifference to any subject apart from querulous complaints about her carers. She had been for many years a dear, generous and entertaining friend, so we all went on being fond of her, and wanting to help, but I'm pretty sure I was not the only one whose sorrow at her death was mingled with relief. And in my case vanity (I suppose) filled me with dismay at the thought of ever inflicting such an experience on my friends.

In the winter of 2008 I went down with flu, and was soon reduced to such a state of inertia that I no longer reached for the glass of water beside my bed, which I knew I ought to be drinking, nor could I summon up the energy to telephone anyone. Eventually a dear friend, Xandra Bingley, happened to telephone me, after which she fed and cared for me with the most generous willingness and good humour until I was better. There was no question of Xandra making heavy weather of it, and I felt nothing but the purest gratitude and relief, but later I remembered that post-Nan dismay. Nan's decline had been gradual, so I had not realized until now that an old person can be reduced to helplessness – can reach the stage of having to be looked after – almost overnight. If I'd had children I suppose I would have accepted, albeit reluctantly, that it could be done by them, but by one's friends? Very occasionally, and if one were able to reciprocate, perhaps; but if it was likely to become more frequent, if it was possible that one might soon become as dependent on their help as Nan had been? No! And how, having reached my nineties, could I fool myself into thinking that I was not moving into that territory? It was then that I decided to call Rose's home and ask them to send me their brochure.

As a result I visited their office and ended by saying that I would like to be considered as a resident if a room came free in about a year's time. I was able to feel that I had made what was probably a sensible decision but was not tied down to it. So for the next twelve months, on the rare occasions when I did think about it, I was able to feel that moving into an old people's home was a comfortably distant event.

By that time I knew a good deal about the home – the Mary Feilding Guild. I learned that the quality of the care was wonderful, and that their rooms were tiny. Visiting Rose, I had not been particularly struck by her room's smallness, I suppose because I had not yet envisaged living in such a room myself, but now I had talked to someone who had just moved in and who was still vividly aware of what she had given up in order to be there, and it was alarming.

You were not, of course, a prisoner in your room. You lunched in the dining room, and at teatime had the choice between a tray in your room or having it in the library. There was also a computer room and various utility rooms, including kitchens with ovens for those who wanted to cook. And the garden was large and very pleasant. It would, I saw, be like going back to boarding school. Except that when you went to school you had no accumulation of possessions to be sacrificed.

It was that which made it such a shock when the letter came saying that a room was now available. It was one of their best rooms, with big windows looking out over the garden and a balcony large enough for several flowerpots and a chair. But it would hold a single bed, a desk, two chairs plus a desk chair – and that was that. The built-in storage space for clothes would hold – perhaps – a quarter of those I possessed; there was only one wall about twelve feet long for pictures. And what would I do about my books?

I came home, sat down in my little sitting room, looked round at the magpie's nest of beloved things accumulated in a long lifetime, and felt: 'But this is *me*.' The extent to which a personality depends on the space it occupies and the objects it possesses appeared to me at that moment overwhelming. How could I perform an act of what amounted to self-destruction? The answer was: *I can't!* I can't and I won't, I'd rather die.

At that stage it would have taken only one word of encouragement from one person, and I would have called the Guild and told them I had changed my mind. I did not get that word. The two people I relied on most for support, my nephew Philip Athill and Xandra, had agreed that in deciding to move to a home I was doing a sensible thing, and I knew both of them felt relief at that decision, as I would have done in their position. Both, when they saw that now I might panic out of it, were perceptibly disturbed at the possibility, again as I would have been. They were not being selfish or unkind. They were simply aware that over their full and busy lives hung the possibility that affection might plunge them into a very onerous responsibility. Of course they didn't want this to happen. It was their reaction that made me suppress the panic.

This horrible feeling came in surges, like fits of nausea – just as excruciating and irresistible, so that while it was going on I was entirely possessed by it; and, like fits of nausea, it passed. It was a relief, gradually to realize this: that what one had to do was hold tight and wait it out, whereupon reason would re-establish its hold: a sensible decision did not become less sensible when it finally led to the action decided on. I must accept that fact, calm down and get on with it.

This became less painful when I discovered to my surprise that getting rid of possessions by giving them to friends or members of my family who would, I was sure, enjoy them turned out to be easy – even a positive pleasure; but unfortunately my books were too many to be disposed of in that way. Some could be given, but most had to be dealt with in bulk. I finally managed it, though just before the final move I experienced a physical collapse serious enough to lead to a night in hospital, which I'm now sure was the result of stress.

The first help came from a very close friend, Sally Bagenal, who swooped in from Kenya for three days and carried me off to buy a bed, an easy chair and a desk (none of the things I possessed would fit into my new room), turning what had looked like a heavy task into an exciting shopping spree. The second help came from my nephew Philip, who hoisted me over the seemingly insurmountable book obstacle. I'd had shelving built in my new room which would hold two or three hundred out of the thousand copies or so that I possessed – but which ones? Every time I tried to decide I sank into a state of shaming uselessness. Philip spent the best part of a day holding up, one by one, every book in that daunting mass and saying, 'In or Out?', then boxing it as appropriate – something which I truly believe I never could have done on my own.

He then took sixteen of my pictures and contrived to hang every one of them (he runs a gallery, so is a master of close-hanging), and on the day of the move, with the help of his son Orlando, went ahead of me, arranged the books on their shelves and my various ornaments in clever places, and made my bed, so the pretty little room had become mine before I set foot in it. I have yet to meet any fellow-resident who had such a good start.

This it was, I believe, that made it possible for me to be so quickly sure that I would be contented here.

~

Newspaper stories about nasty happenings in homes for old people, when untrained, probably underpaid and obviously ill-chosen staff have bullied and manhandled helpless residents, have been shocking, but no more so to us, who are residents in such a home, than to outsiders. Being old ourselves, we naturally feel for the victims, but apart from that, such stories have nothing to do with us. Our home – and no doubt the same could be said of many others – is one in which such happenings are unthinkable. Basically, this is because ours is not one of the many run for profit.

Ours is run by a charity founded in 1876 by Lady Mary Feilding (not a spelling mistake), the eldest daughter of the Earl of Denbigh, with the help of God. Whatever one's own feeling about God, it would be a mistake to belittle Lady Mary's, because her unwavering belief in Him shaped her whole life, and did a great deal to shape ours. She never made any decision without a period of earnest prayer, and the many decisions she had to make in the course of organizing what came to be called the Mary Feilding Guild all turned out to be wise and practical. No doubt, when putting them into practice, being the daughter of an earl was also helpful. It is not likely that the daughter of a country parson, still less of a baker or a blacksmith, even if as genuinely pious as Lady Mary, could have persuaded so many rich and important people to contribute support to the cause she favoured.

She had identified a crying need: working gentlewomen whose working days were over. At that time no gentlewoman would have been working for her living if she had any family to support her, nor would she have had the training for the kind of work which enabled her to earn enough money to accumulate savings. She would almost always have been a governess, and only very rarely would her employers have loved her enough to keep her on for free until she died. For such unfortunate women it was a case of job over, food and shelter gone.

The Guild helped such women in many different ways. God saw to it that Lady Mary was supplied with shrewd financial advice (letters reveal that whenever someone helpful turned up she was certain that God had sent him or her). As time went by and the nature of society changed, the Guild's nature changed too, until it ended up with a considerable chunk of valuable property on which stands the present home, now described as 'A Retirement Home for the Active Elderly', which takes men as well as women. The residents now pay for their keep, although a good deal less than they would in any other comfortable and well-run retirement home; and no one has ever been asked to leave on account of running out of money. A fund exists to deal with such an emergency. It is not a nursing home, but care is available as and when it becomes needed, up to any point at which hospital treatment has to be resorted to. The ideal is that we should go on living in our rooms until we die.

There is one important respect in which Lady Mary's touch, in spite of all the changes, can still be felt. She was always strict about respect: the people being helped by the Guild must never feel humiliated. And this rule of hers has been faithfully preserved by generation after generation of her successors. Residents must always be addressed by their surnames and titles; their rooms must be absolutely theirs, no one entering must forget to knock; they must be free to come and go as they wish, leading their lives in a way as normal as their health permits. And in addition to this civilized respect for the residents, there is obviously great care taken in the employment of the staff, who genuinely like old people. Soon after I arrived I said to one of them that I'd been surprised to discover how interesting one very old resident, who looked as though she was almost past communication, turned out to be. 'Oh,' she replied, 'I think everyone here is interesting if you take the trouble to get to know them.' And I have now been here five years without ever coming across any exception to this pleasing attitude; and on the few occasions when I have been less than well, the comfort of being kindly looked after was inexpressible.

Being free to live as one wishes does sometimes have unexpected results. One of the four women with whom I shared a table at lunch when I first arrived – I shall call her Hildegard – struck me as a forceful character. She wore bright coloured dresses which dated from the 1960s, and on hearing that I was still driving, said briskly, 'Good. You can take me to Kew.' The drive from Highgate to Kew, across pretty well the full width of London, could scarcely be more tiresome, so I said equally briskly that no, I couldn't, and was relieved when she accepted my rudeness calmly. Someone then told me that Hildegard, though spindly and with one paralysed arm, travelled to India every summer, managing the journey by ruthlessly telling people to help her and not wasting energy by minding if they failed to respond. My friend added rather oddly: 'Have you seen Hildegard's room?' This was a question that I was asked by several other people, so eventually I went to see why . . . and it was worth the expedition. The room was so crammed with bags, boxes and small pieces of furniture that it was literally impossible to see where her bed was: each night she must have had to dig her way into it. I could distinguish the presence of a large and rather beautiful dolls' house and several teddy bears, and there seemed to be a chest of drawers against one wall. 'But Hildegard,' I said, 'how on earth do you get things in or out of that?' 'Oh, that,' she replied. 'I haven't opened that for eight years.' She then scrambled her way to the door into her shower room and shoved it ajar – it wouldn't open any further – and that little room was stuffed from wall to wall and floor to ceiling. (Hildegard was not dirty. Every corridor has extra lavatories and spare bathrooms for those who dislike showers.) The normal procedure here is that our rooms are cleaned for us once a week. Hildegard's room could never have been cleaned, which must, in the past, have distressed the cleaning staff. They had, however, got used to it. This was how Hildegard liked it, so that was that: an attitude which I found wholly admirable. And which, alas, I am not sure that we could count on today. Our management does its best to fight free of the web of red tape woven by authorities in their attempts to guard against horrors in care homes (attempts that are necessary and laudable, but can verge on the over-careful); but it would be a miracle if they could always win.

Those teddy bears of Hildegard's: they pushed me into a faux pas. I discovered that they were not the only ones – indeed, that from time to time a teddy-bears' picnic was held in the library, and was well attended. 'How very odd,' I said to Mary, next to whom I sat at lunch, 'how really very odd it is that so many old women still treasure their teddy bears,' and I fear that I must have smirked. Her smile was slightly vague. And a few days later, passing the open door of her room, what did I see but a procession of five little teddy bears on a window sill, and on her bed . . . a pink plush elephant. What made this even odder was that Mary, without telling any of us, had for many years been working away at a very thoroughly researched biography of Robespierre's younger brother – an alarmingly boring man – which we learnt about only when its publication was announced a few weeks before her death. After reading a biography of Jung I had concluded that psychiatrists were people who could make a little nuttiness go a very long way. This opinion was confirmed when I learnt that both Hildegard and Mary were retired psychiatrists.

On hearing where I now live, people often say, 'Isn't that the home which won't take you unless you can read Proust in French?' – a joke we find tedious. A lot of us are North Londoners and all of us had to be able to raise enough money to keep ourselves here for at least most of our old age, so we tend to be reasonably well-educated middle-class people with a wide variety of backgrounds. Five years ago, when I arrived, there were no men among us. At present there are two, one a retired doctor, the other an entomologist (ants were, I believe, his speciality, but he knows a great deal about a lot of other things as well). The dearth of men is at least partly explained by widows living longer than widowers, and widowed men being more likely to be scooped up by single women than the other way round, owing to the weakness so many women have for looking after the helpless and/or being married come what may. (Having tasted the delights of being utterly free of any domestic responsibilities, I find that weakness very hard to understand.)

The independence allowed us by this place has much to be said for it, in addition to our being treated as adult human beings. It makes it easy for us to keep ourselves to ourselves if that is what we want to do, so that living here is less like being back at school than it seemed at first. That and a twinge of dismay at being surrounded by so many old people were the two worries that hovered over my first week here, only to be quickly dispersed. The likeness to being at a boarding school can't be wholly denied, but is very superficial, and alarm at so much oldness is simply resentment of one's own old age – something one gets used to because of having no alternative. Anyone here who persists in it soon begins to seem absurd. Not having to be sociable as a condition for being here results in slow gravitation towards congenial people, leading to real friendships. During the year when I was waiting to hear from the Guild that they had a room for me – the time when my decision had been made but I didn't yet know what it involved – I thought quite often that I would not necessarily lose touch with my old friends, but I can't remember expecting to make new ones. That, however, has happened.

Old-age friendships are slightly different from those made in the past, which consisted largely of sharing whatever happened to be going on. What happens to be going on for us now is waiting to die, which is of course a bond of a sort, but lacks the element of enjoyability necessary to friendship. In my current friendships I find that element not in our present circumstances but in excursions into each other's pasts. A shared sense of humour is necessary, together with some degree of curiosity. Given those, we become for each other wonderfully interesting stories, which arouse genuine concern, admiration and affection. To begin with I thought, 'My word, this house is bursting with stories! Someone – me? – ought to go round with a tape recorder, collecting them.' But then I realized that what I was calling 'stories' were – of course! – lives still being lived, not material for entertainment. They must be revealed only by those living them, brought forth only by warmth, sympathy and mutual esteem, as the material of friendship.

As examples, two of the women I have come to know best. It is a pity that the word 'dainty' has become suspect, because restored to its dictionary meaning – 'delicate, elegant, graceful, pretty, refined, scrupulous' – it is precisely the right word for

Minna, who arrived here on the same day as I did, 15 December 2009. She was born in the East End of London to an overworked, short-tempered mother and at a very early age had the care of six younger siblings dumped on her shoulders. At the age of eleven she tried to run away from this uneasy home, knocking on doors to ask for work (she got no further than two streets away). The one thing she always knew was that she wanted to learn, and being apprenticed to a firm of milliners did not assuage this need. Luckily, however, she discovered Toynbee Hall, the East End organization that saved so many young people like her, and it became what she describes as 'one of my universities'. She had to go further afield to find the other one.

Like many Jewish families, hers was scattered widely. It included an aunt who lived in Cape Town, ran a millinery business, and offered to take Minna on. I think she was seventeen when she arrived in Cape Town, to be greeted rather fiercely by the aunt, who turned out to be disconcertingly like her mother, and put to work selling hats to Boer ladies whose accents she couldn't understand and whose names she couldn't spell. Quite soon, however, she heard of a group of people who met regularly to listen to records of classical music, and there she caught the eye of a rather older man, a pharmacist. Almost at once he proposed to her (she must have been irresistible – tiny, with a halo of golden hair and the most transparent delicacy of mind and heart) – and she, shocked, refused him because she was sure that everyone would believe that, being penniless, she was marrying him for his money. It took him all of three weeks to overcome this principled resistance. She then discovered that as well as knowing a great deal about music, he could never go out without dropping into a bookshop, and never leave a bookshop without at least two new books in his pocket, and thus began her second 'university'. Their children grew up to be clever and successful, and Minna is certainly among the best-read women in this place, as well as being a gifted water-colourist and a most discriminating listener to music. But what is most remarkable about her is her absolutely unshakeable, though very quiet, honesty and integrity.

By an odd coincidence, my second 'example', Rita, also came to England from South Africa, with an exceptionally intelligent and able husband. Her father had the foresight to move his family from Vienna to Cape Town before they absolutely had to take such a step, so Rita's girlhood was spent happily in that beautiful place, and it was there that her husband became a successful barrister. They came to England with two small children because his opposition to apartheid was threatening him with serious trouble, in spite of the fact that he would not be able to practise here without starting again from scratch. They had no friends here, so he had to turn his hand at once to uncongenial jobs, and she too had to find work where she could, while raising the children. Their struggle resulted in their becoming an extraordinarily close-knit family. While it was going on it must have felt not only hard, but very long. In retrospect, however, their successful establishment in this country looks surprisingly quick and complete, and clearly this was largely because of Rita's energy, optimism, and openness to new experiences and new people. If Rita finds a new restaurant it is not just good, it is beautiful, and new friends are lovely people, and they stay lovely too, because she is tireless in keeping her many and varied friendships in good repair. Her generosity is unfailing. One of the younger residents in this place, Rita still drives her car, and whisks people off on shopping excursions and so on at the drop of a hat. She also follows a wide range of interests and goes regularly to a jazz club, a creative-writing class, a poetry-reading group and a discussion group run by the University of the Third Age, and she has organized a debating society within our home. She makes me feel lazy, in spite of kindly making more allowances than I do myself for the difference between our ages, and she has allowed me very rewarding access to her family.

And these are only two of the people whose company I enjoy in this place, and who have added considerably to the interest of my own life. As has the company of other people who, like me, miss their gardens a great deal.

My balcony overlooks the lawn, with beyond it the gardens and trees of the other houses in the street – Highgate is a bosky place. There is a magnolia tree as high as the house just outside my window, with a large and floriferous Japanese crab apple just beyond it. To start with I could potter about in the garden, and even plant things, provided I didn't offend the gardeners. I gathered that the place had been a jungle until the Guild had found them, man and wife, an incredibly hard-working pair who come only once a week and somehow manage to keep the place spick and span. Given the chance, I fear I *would* have offended them, because their passion for tidiness makes them too severe with shrubs, which they chop ruthlessly into square or doughnut shapes regardless of their nature, which deeply offends me, and also the other ex-gardeners among the residents.

We began to mutter, but only mildly and between ourselves, until the arrival of a new resident, who moved into the room next to mine: Elva, quite young (only in her mid-eighties), energetic, in no way institutionalized, who saw no reason why we shouldn't ask for what we wanted. Look, she said, there's all that long narrow bit behind the house which is a horrid mess (it had been neglected because it is rather shady): why shouldn't we be given that to develop and be allowed to garden it ourselves? Why not, indeed; Elva had identified four people who, like her, were still capable of hands-on gardening. They didn't, alas, include me because by now I have become too physically wobbly to be of any use, so all that I could contribute was enthusiasm and a few ideas. She also had an ally in Vera, who some years ago had successfully won the right to garden a square flower bed near a door into the house, and a long narrow one beside the path leading to it, and who still does garden that bit successfully in spite of deteriorating eyesight. After a short campaign, we were granted the shady garden to be our very own, and were free to discover that the soil was a mixture of clay and builder's rubble. Undeterred, Elva contributed a tremendously sturdy and kind grandson, appropriately named Hector, who set to and dug out three large barrowfuls of brick, and gardening began.

It then occurred to me that although I couldn't *do* anything, I could buy some plants. There is a little narrow bed near the start of our area, which I thought would look good with six roses in it. Those I offered to buy, and the others liked the idea well enough to help me to pay for the roses, which arrived bare-rooted from David Austen's last November. There were six large holes waiting for them, dug by kind able-bodied people – which had revealed that although that bed contained no bricks it was composed of the vilest clay, made more forbidding by the fact that the plants' arrival had been preceded by a week of heavy rain. There was, however, nowhere else to put them, so we had to hope that if we added a lot of compost when we planted them, they would survive. The team was asked to stand by for planting after lunch.

Only three of us turned up. Elva had a hospital appointment that day and the others simply forgot, something only too likely to happen at any event in a home for old people. No one was there but nearly blind Vera, aged ninety-four, Pamela, also ninety-four, and me, three weeks before my ninety-seventh birthday . . . which really amounted to being just Pamela, because although she's the same age as Vera, she is slim and amazingly nimble for her age. It was Vera who said, 'Let's try to get one of them in, at least,' but it could only be Pamela who got down on her knees – squelch, squelch in that sodden clay – to spread out the rose's roots at the bottom of the hole. I then did the sprinkling of nourishing rose food, Vera did the tipping of compost out of a bucket, and Vera and I then jointly scraped clay back into the hole before hoisting Pamela to her feet (no one in this place can get up once down) so that she could tread the plant in. Whereupon Pamela's shoes came off, and from being merely gallant she became heroic. Shoving her mud-caked feet into her squelchy shoes, she said, 'Well, we've done that one so we might as well do another.' *And we ended by doing all six.* By the time we tottered back to our rooms we were too exhausted to speak, but we were very pleased with ourselves. One good thing about being physically incapable of doing almost anything is that if you manage to do even a little something, you feel great. And I can report that all six rose bushes have begun, five months after being planted, to develop buds.

Plenty of entertainment is offered by the Guild – concerts, talks, exercise classes, poetry and discussion groups and films, shown in the library at weekends, none of which is obligatory. Before the election this year all four of the local candidates were lined up in our dining room to answer our questions. All that is valuable, and so is the luxury of being free of domestic worries and knowing that kind care is available if one needs it; but nothing is more valuable than being free to do whatever you are capable of doing. That is why I, having made the right decision, am most grateful to Mary Feilding's successors, and her God.

A Life of Luxuries

As a child I knew exactly what was most desirable: pinkness and sparkle. When I was grown-up I was going to sweep down a flight of stairs into a great ballroom wearing a pink satin dress with a huge skirt: yards and yards of the shiniest pink satin, because obviously if something was desirable you couldn't have too much of it. Oh, scrumptious pinkness! It must have been what princesses wore. In those days – I was born in 1917 – we had no television and newspapers didn't reach the nursery, so my idea of glamour came from illustrated fairy stories. The princesses in these books went in for the beautiful and rich; they always had flowing hair and lovely robes. A princess was what I was going to be, with coal-black hair I could sit on. (There was a rather depressing day when I was about eleven, when I stood in front of the bathroom mirror and, looking at myself, faced the fact that, although of course I was going to change as I grew up, I was never going to change to the point of having coal-black hair that I could sit on. I was a mouse-coloured child.)

Then dresses became real. They were made by my clever mother and entailed standing up straight and not fidgeting while she tweaked and pinned. They were never of pink satin, which I came to understand was just as well. We didn't often bother with day dresses because in the daytime country children like us, growing up in darkest Norfolk, wore boringly practical garments: Aertex shirts and linen skirts. When we were a bit older we moved on to suits (we called them 'coats and skirts'), of tweed in the winter and of grey flannel in the summer, which were made by a tailor in Norwich. Choosing the tweed was fun. My mother and I avoided the tailor's boring selection (except, of course, for riding clothes); instead we used to go to Southwold, where an adventurous couple had set up a loom and made tweeds in unusual and attractive colours. This upset the tailor, but did not prevent him from making a faultless garment. I had two; one was a very smart dark blue and black plaid, and the other was a soft rust-red. They were comfortable and lasted for ever. And because we didn't live in London, and hardly ever went there, we never saw anybody wearing anything different. You didn't desire what you didn't know about.

In my teens, there were a great many tennis parties and dances. We had plenty of friends – but no one whom one knew very intimately, no one with whom we would have had conversation about anything that mattered. (We had cousins for that.) There were two beautiful girls called Diana and Camilla, who seemed to me exquisitely sophisticated. They wore make-up long before any of the rest of us and had plucked eyebrows – in those days there was a fashion that you plucked your eyebrows to a single line – and I remember thinking Camilla's plucked eyebrows the height of elegance, and feeling both envious and humbled by them. My mother allowed powdering the nose and a bit of lipstick from quite early, but not eyebrow plucking.

The dresses my mother made were for parties – soon, dances. For those, you wore things in which you could become someone nearer your dream self, so you could hope to be fallen in love with. I still think fondly of my mother's creations: she had taught herself to be good at dressmaking; they never looked in the least homemade. When I was about seventeen, there was a silver-grey velvet with a wonderfully full skirt which I adored, and a beautiful French taffeta, sea-blue with the finest of black lines, for which she devised a broad hem of black velvet which made all the difference. And when I insisted, at twenty and by then studying at Oxford, on having my first black dress she found a tulle with coin-sized shiny dots on it which was just the thing. She made it in two parts. Underneath there was a close-fitting sheath, over it a tunic of tulle held in at the waist and with fitted sleeves. As I then had, believe it or not, a twenty-two-inch waist, in the evening I generally specialized in tight bodices and full skirts, but this was straight up and down – an exciting change.

I can't help regretting the passing of the evening dress – what in my mother's young days was called a ball gown – because almost any woman moves better and looks prettier in a floor-length dress, with her shoulders emerging from beautiful material. I think its demise came about when the word 'sexy' became acceptable as a description of an attractive garment. It was not that young women in the past were any less eager than those of today to make men desire them, but the words we associated with desirability were 'beauty', 'prettiness', 'charm'. I remember the first time I heard 'sexy' applied with approval to a piece of clothing – which would have been in the 1950s; it surprised me a bit. Because it was said by a Canadian, I thought it was probably natural as a transatlantic usage, although a bit odd – well, vulgar-sounding – to English ears. It was applied to a very chic piece of beach-wear she was kindly offering to lend me: a pair of three-quarter-length black linen cigarette trousers and a wide-necked top that stood away from your shoulders with a turned-over collar. It was very becoming and I was delighted to borrow it, so she can't have been meaning anything rude.

In our 'pre-sexy' days, from childhood and right through the war years, *Vogue* was our bible, both for inspiration and for its patterns. My favourite occupation (after riding, reading and dancing) was poring over its pages, imagining that God had told me that I must choose one thing off every page, although that game was nearer bitter than sweet because it always ended by knowing I could never afford any of them. My family could afford to educate us and keep us decently dressed until we could earn our own livings, but they were always anxious about money. Never was it possible to spend light-heartedly, and still less could I do that once I was out on my own.

But still I wanted to wear dresses bought from a shop. I think I was about fifteen when I saw the gold lamé evening dress in the window of a Norwich boutique. Its hem was trimmed with mink, and so was its off-the-shoulder neckline, and although I knew perfectly well a fifteen-year-old girl would look worse than comic in it, I yearned for it, or rather, to be the person who could wear it. The truth was that never, on the rare occasions when I achieved a shop dress, was it as pretty as any of those made by my mother, because always the excitement of choosing made me lose my head. The worst time was when, because the occasion was so important, I was allowed to go to London and choose the dress I was to be presented in. In those days, daughters of families like mine were presented at court – or rather, this time, at a garden party. It was 1936, during the very brief period when Edward was on the throne before bolting to marry Mrs Simpson, and he had evidently gone on strike at the prospect of the traditional evening event at which the debutantes would wear evening dresses with trains, and feathers in their hair. That was a bit disappointing, because a long day dress plus a hat was less exotic, but still it was an Event – so why did I come away from the elegant shop into which I had gone so timidly with a dress in the one colour that I knew didn't suit me: green? I hated (and still hate) green – not as a colour, but on me. And what was more, though it was made of tulle, full-length, close-fitting but with big leg-of-mutton sleeves and a flick outwards at the bottom, I knew that wearing it with long black gloves and a wide black hat was not going to help. I have a vivid memory of the mask of desperate boredom on the sulky little royal countenance, glimpsed as I bobbed my curtsey. I was not far from feeling the same.

This was the same year when at eighteen, I started at Lady Margaret Hall. There was no particular dress code for the girls at Oxford, and chiefly I wore my two tweed suits; though I owned a pair of trousers by then, I didn't think of wearing them for anything other than messing about in the country. I also bought a long white coat in a guinea shop – shops where everything cost a guinea, or twenty-one shillings – which was very dashing; it must have been a success because one day when I was walking through the park at Oxford a lady said to me: 'May I say, how pretty you look.' What I really longed for was a fur coat. A sable fur coat – not because it would be warm, but because it would be elegant, like Katharine Hepburn was elegant (I didn't quite aspire to Dietrich or Garbo, who I thought were absolutely the very top of beauty, but unreachable). My dear mother managed to scrape up the money to give me a musquash coat on my twenty-first birthday. I tried very hard not to feel disappointed, but never quite succeeded.

In 1939, I graduated. My independence coincided with the beginning of the Second World War, so there were six years ahead in which fashion froze and no one was allowed more clothing coupons than could provide for bare necessities. My first job was clerking for a branch of the Admiralty, in Bath, where it was camped for the duration. Later I worked in London for the BBC's Empire Service. I made a very great friend who lived nearby and she and I used to pore over the pages of *Vogue* together, just as I had done as a child – but really fashion was irrelevant. Everything was so hellish, one didn't even think about it. I wore my two tweed suits and little else; what would have felt like a luxury to me then was food. Really delicious food.

After the war's end Dior's New Look came creeping through from Paris, wildly exciting, even if, like me, you could hope to achieve no more than an approximation to it. Like everyone else, I began to look like a woman again. But at the same time I had also become grown-up, was loving my job in publishing and soon would be sharing my life with a man who would not have noticed if I was wearing a sack with holes in it for my head and arms. He had accepted the fact that if a woman was going to a party she took off the dress she had been wearing and put on another, but he hadn't a clue why she did it, so saw no reason why he should be interested, and since we were getting on very well together, I saw no reason to try to change him. This, combined with the fact that although you could make a living publishing books it was only a modest one, meant that I had entered a part of my life – a large part of it – in which clothes were not important.

There was a certain unspoken dress code for working women, but what you wore to work was very little different from what you wore at home; it was part of what one was. I seem to remember wearing a good deal of beige, and my lack of confidence in shopping turned into positive dislike. I had a friend to whom going shopping in the company of another woman was apparently a treat, and I knew she was not alone in enjoying this – in fact it was quite likely that more women were like her than like me. But her taste for it remained as mysterious to me as women's attitude to clothes was to my old man.

During these years when clothes were not important to me I was not entirely indifferent to them. I no longer took *Vogue*, but something in me kept an eye on fashion: I didn't follow it, but I always knew where it was going. And I was not above being riveted when, on one occasion during the 1960s, I saw a stunningly elegant woman. I was in a shop which sold expensive foods, buying a special cheese, when in came this arresting vision. She was small, perhaps Japanese but not obviously so, and everything about her – her coat, in a rather difficult yellow, her exquisite little shoes, hat, handbag – was unique, in some way unlike anything I had seen before, but perfect to the last stitch; as was every hair under the perfect hat and every touch of make-up on her totally impassive face. As by then women were on the whole wearing rather casual clothes, she really was odd, as if she'd come out of another world. The woman behind the counter and I gazed at her in astonishment, and when she left the shop with her little parcel, looking as though she were enclosed and protected by an invisible bubble of pure elegance, we turned to each other, round-eyed. 'Who is she?' I asked. 'I've never seen her before – she must be someone famous,' was the awestruck reply; and the odd thing about this vision was that she was creepy rather than enviable. I remember thinking: 'It's impossible to imagine her in bed with a man.' I didn't – yes, I was quite sure I didn't – want to be like her. But she had reminded me that there was a dream . . .

And there were some interesting clothes going on. Ossie Clark and Celia Birtwell's long peasanty dresses, for instance. But I never went near them – much as I would have liked to – because of money. I did do that sort of hippy look: you either wore mini skirts or maxi skirts, and I wore maxis. Rather dashingly, I wore more maxi than anyone else in the office. I liked that. Just once I was tempted to buy a dress by Jean Muir, and tried one on in Harvey Nichols – a lovely plain blue in a very fine silk knit – but it was hopeless, it clung in all the wrong places, and was very much nicer in the hand than it was on. I didn't buy it.

What restored my feeling for clothes was being released from visiting shops by mail order, the development of which coincided with my professional Indian summer. As middle age began to slide towards being old, I started to make some unexpected money by writing. As I reached my eighties, mail order (which I used to despise because early catalogues specialized in woolly vests and old ladies' bedroom slippers) began displaying real clothes. And leafing through catalogues felt familiar. It felt enjoyable. It felt almost like leafing through *Vogue* used to feel. And very soon I discovered Wall, which every season produces at least one thing – a pair of trousers, an oversize shirt for when one has to bypass the waist – which I have to have, even when it costs more than I have ever spent before, so that whenever I fall for Wall I am consumed by sensations of guilt. And thus I have made a most interesting discovery: everything I have bought as a result of a guilt-inspiring impulse has been a success. This also applies on the rare occasions when I venture out of mail order. There is a designer of magical knitwear called Anne Higgins who used to sell by exhibiting her work here or there on rare occasions, letting customers know by postcard, but now has a tiny boutique in Kensington; and there is a corner of the Victoria & Albert Museum shop which displays clothes. At both of these I have proved the truth of the Infallibility of the Guilty Impulse, so that now my wardrobe can hardly recognize itself.

This revival happened just in time, because when one has become very old, which I take to mean over ninety-five, one's idea of luxury shifts away from clothes. I do still own, and occasionally wear, a beautiful printed coat-dress in dark blue and white cotton, with a Javanese print and sky-blue lining, and little fabric buttons all the way down; and also a lovely black jacket patterned with circles of many-coloured material appliquéd by clever Indian hands (that came from the V&A). But my main luxury is now something which many misguided old people dread: the wheelchair. They think submitting to it is humiliating, and they are wrong. Nothing could be more deliciously luxurious than being pushed around a really thrilling and crowded exhibition in a wheelchair. The crowd falls away on either side like the Red Sea parting for the Israelites, and there you are, lounging in front of the painting of your choice in perfect comfort. I shall never forget the first time I fully realized how marvellous this can be. It was in front of Matisse's red *Dance*, and I have never enjoyed a great painting more intensely.

Lessons

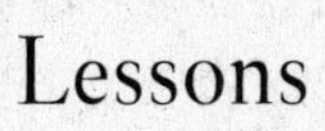

The things life teaches you are not always valuable. Many people learn not to trust, not to hope, not to give. But if you are lucky in your circumstances – have loving parents, are spared extreme poverty or early exposure to loss, violence or frustration – and if you are equipped with a reasonable amount of natural wit, the chances are that what it teaches will be useful. I, for example, am convinced that two of the things I've learnt have contributed a great deal to the fact that, looking back on my life, I see it as being, in spite of various setbacks, a happy one.

My two valuable lessons are: avoid romanticism and abhor possessiveness. Both of these can be dangerous, and in conjunction with sexuality even lethal. The first has plunged innumerable couples into disappointing, sometimes disastrous, marriages, and it is far from uncommon for the second to cause horrors such as a man choosing to murder his wife rather than see her prefer the company of another man. And even well short of such an extreme result, it can and often does cause a great deal of distress and pain.

It was fairly easy for me to learn both these lessons because I have a prosaic personality and little natural inclination towards possessiveness, but it is far from easy for many people. Some even consider attitudes which I think poisonous to be necessary or beautiful, and it would be naïve to imagine that argument could change their minds. Probably the best one can hope for is that romanticism and possessiveness should be less often taught by what the young read, sing and see on screens.

This is not the place to go into detailed autobiography (plenty of which I have done elsewhere), but my beliefs were learnt from my own experience, so that experience has to be sketched in. I can say, therefore, that the most valuable relationship of my life lasted for forty-odd years because neither my partner nor I was possessive. Nor were we romantic. We just happened to know each other well enough to talk and listen without inhibition, and to recognize that we could do this from our first meeting, which appears to me to be the necessary bedrock for love. What Barry and I had between us began when I was forty-three, passed through years of sexual harmony and others of solid friendship, and ended only when he became too ill and I (approaching my ninetieth birthday) too old for us to carry on. At that point, luckily for both of us, he was rescued by a loving niece who swooped in and carried him off to spend his last days in his native Jamaica. My body recognized my relief at this before my mind did. For months I had been enduring a lot of pain from what I thought was rheumatism. Three weeks after he left I suddenly realized that the pain had disappeared.

Quite unlike this relationship was one that hit me when I was twenty-three and extremely vulnerable because I was recovering from heartbreak. I had fallen in love at the age of fifteen with Tony, to whom I became engaged when I was seventeen. That, suprisingly, was a sensible love because we suited each other well. The snag was that he was a person who lived in the moment with unusual intensity, which made him wonderful to be with but dangerous to be apart from, and apart we were when he, who was in the Air Force, was posted to Egypt, and I decided that I was enjoying my last year at Oxford too much to give it up, so that instead of getting married before he left we would wait until that year was over. And then the Second World War began. Knowing him as I did, I could never blame him for falling in love with a girl who was in his present moment, but I did suffer greatly from the way in which he abandoned me by simply going silent, without explanation, for two years. It was a miserable ordeal and felt like the end of everything, because I had never foreseen any future for myself other than marriage: it seemed as though I had lost my life as well as my love.

After leaving university I was living at home in Norfolk with my mother (my father was away in the Army). I was doing my best to lead a normal existence, but it was difficult because none of the men I met had any quality apart from 'not being Tony'. I had a strong feeling of being 'dead'.

Our house was on the estate of my maternal grandparents, just across the park from their much larger house, which had been taken over by the Army for the duration of the war and now sheltered a shifting population of soldiers being trained for active service. We felt, as everyone did, that we must be hospitable to the officers in charge of those soldiers, dumped as the poor fellows were far from their homes and families, to live in considerable discomfort with people not necessarily of their choice, prior to being sent off to God knew where and the possibility of death. So my mother and I did what we felt to be our duty, and invited the major in charge to come across the park and have supper with us.

The man who appeared, called Stephen, was in his mid to late forties, extremely tall, good-looking, and – it soon appeared – from a background similar to our own: country people, but civilized country people, whose involvement with their horses and dogs didn't prevent their houses from being full of books. He was Irish, but his job in peacetime had been housemaster in one of the smaller English public schools. He was easy to talk to, and obviously pleased to have been rescued from loneliness by people who turned out to be congenial. I suppose about half an hour passed before I realized that perhaps this was a man who was not just 'not Tony'. We were due to go a day or two later to a small dance being given by friends of ours who lived twelve miles away, and I was pleased when my mother asked him if he would like to come with us. Yes, he would; and I, who had been feeling pretty tepid about that dance, began to look forward to it.

We spent a lot of that evening dancing together, and by the end of it his 'not being Tony' was completely replaced by his being Stephen; and I – oh God, how wonderful: I was not feeling dead any more!

My mother was driving that evening, and a friend of hers had come with us, so it was natural that on the homeward journey Stephen and I should sit in the back of the car. At once his presence beside me became electric and I could feel my hand, which was resting on the seat between us, begin to hum with invitation. I was careful not to make any provocative movement, but that very care seemed to increase the intensity of the humming, so that I was hardly surprised when his hand reached out to cover mine. Mine turned over so that we were palm to palm, and the shock of it was like that of two naked bodies meeting. After a couple of minutes he withdrew his hand – oh no! – but it was only to slip his arm round me and draw me closer, so there I was, talking lightly to the two women in the front seats as though nothing was happening, while this secret rapture was melting my bones. There wasn't a shadow of doubt, from that moment on, that we would soon be making love.

I suppose Stephen must have been thinking, probably with amusement, something on the lines of, 'Well I never, this apparently respectable girl isn't half ready for it!'; but as the affair developed he must have realized that I had fallen wildly, abjectly in love with him. There began to be a gentleness, even a tenderness, in his behaviour that suggested as much. He clearly was not a man accustomed to having affairs. To this day I can remember every significant word he spoke to me: after our first love-making – 'Oh my God, I'd forgotten I could feel like this'; after he'd been back to Ireland on a week's leave – 'I thought of you all the time, even at the most unsuitable moments'; during our last love-making – 'I don't suppose you'll believe this, but I do love you'. I wished he hadn't made that last remark, because he was right: I didn't believe him. Or rather, I said to myself, 'When he says "love" he doesn't mean what I am feeling.' But I never dreamt of telling him what I was feeling. I never asked or told him anything, because I didn't feel I had the right to. If I asked I would be intruding on forbidden territory, and if I told I would be burdening him with unwelcome information. That was what I felt. I suppose it was because he was so much older than I was, and his being married made him, in my eyes, a different kind of person.

Because I knew quite soon that he was married. I'd had to go to London for two days and on one of those days my mother had spent an evening with him. Although I had thought I was being cleverly discreet, I don't doubt that she could see my enraptured condition only too clearly. When I got home she said: 'Darling, you do know that Stephen is married, don't you?' 'Yes, of course,' I snapped, and went quickly out of the room before (so I hoped) she could see I was lying. Shutting myself into the lavatory, I thought: 'What now? I suppose I ought to stop this quickly, before it becomes impossible?' And the answer came instantly: 'I'm not going to. It will end in tears but so what, I don't care. I simply don't care. *Nothing on earth is going to make me give this up!'*

Our affair was short, a matter of a few embraces in the backs of cars and on woodland walks, and only two blissful nights in bed together, before the Army spirited him away to who knows where (wartime destinations were always strictly secret), after which only two letters and a sadness that was made more shattering by my mother finding out everything. (Fortunately I was able quickly to find a job that took me away from home, thereby allowing my mother and me eventually to recover our mutual love.)

I never dared to suppose that Stephen would think of getting a divorce and asking me to marry him, but if he had done so I would certainly have said yes, and if he survived the war (oh, how I hope he did) that wonderful, awe-inspiring being would have turned into an Irish schoolmaster in the most boring kind of school, and I would have become a schoolmaster's wife. And that, very probably, would have ended in disaster. Such speculation is, of course, idle, but I was going to learn for a fact that I am not good wife material, so I can't deny that it could have happened.

I used to suppose that my unwifeliness was the result of suffering early and discouraging misfortunes in my love life, and those may indeed have contributed to it; but now I think that I could not have slid into it so easily and totally without discomfort unless there had been an innate disposition towards it. There had always been a lack of the maternal instinct. As a child I despised dolls, and later I remember thinking, when looking at a small baby, 'I'd much rather pick up a puppy.' That shocked me. Tony had enjoyed imagining the children we would have, and I had recognized my own lack of enthusiasm for this game, but not how deep it went. I quickly told myself, after the puppy incident, that once I had a child of my own no doubt I would love it: that must be how it worked, so stop worrying. Perhaps I was right about that. Perhaps. It is true that when, in my forties, my body tricked me into pregnancy I did experience intense happiness, but to this day I am disconcerted by the speed with which I recovered from the miscarriage. I expected something far worse than the one dreary little dream I had, soon after leaving the hospital, and I have never had a single wistful thought about that child. I suspect that a streak of beady-eyed detachment that I can detect in myself steers me away from very strong emotional commitment. The role that seems to me most comfortable is not that of Wife, but that of the Other Woman. And in that role I am good, because I have never for a moment expected or wanted to wreck anyone's marriage.

What I was really happy with was a lover who had a nice wife to do his washing and look after him if he fell ill, so that I could enjoy the plums of love without having to munch through the pudding. That was what I had during the first eight years of my relationship with Barry. As soon as his wife divorced him and the munching began, clouds began to gather, to be dispersed in a way which must have appeared to onlookers a bit odd. I ceased to want him as a lover, he found someone else who did, she moved in with us and became my best and closest friend, which she still is, and for the next six years we three lived together as happy as can be. She – Sally – was much younger than we were, so eventually she decided to move out and get married. By that time we were so firmly knitted together as 'family' that we didn't lose her – we simply absorbed her husband – and in the years that followed they and their two children could be relied on to help us keep going. Because gradually we did need helping. Barry's health began to fail and as he got iller and iller, I got older and older. By the time my ninetieth birthday was approaching, looking after him ... well, I remember thinking, 'Talk about munching! I might just as well have been a wife after all.' It is blood-chilling to think of all the old couples who have to plough on together without our luck.

That luck consisted partly of the support we received from our beloved 'family', and finally even more from the generosity of Barry's family. When he was rescued by them, so was I.

Those long years we spent together were, in spite of their sad end, thoroughly rewarding as far as I was concerned. During them I was able to enjoy a relationship while living my own life and discovering myself, as I don't think I could have done in an ordinary marriage, where very often a woman's happiness, or at least contentment, has to be won by learning to shape herself into a good fit in another person's life. And a marriage plunged into while blinded by an abject romantic passion such as mine for Stephen ... well, one can't be sure, but I would certainly never bet on its working well. So, when my mother told me that

Stephen was married, ought I to have erased the possibility of disaster by being sensible? Am I sorry that I didn't do that?

No, I am not. Everything I say about how my life developed is true, but still, without the memory of that delicious passion, it would have been much the poorer. So much for the wisdom of old age!

Beloved Books

My mother used to state that she disliked poetry and was bored by Shakespeare, which was shocking in a granddaughter of a Master of an Oxford college, raised in a house full of books. As a girl I was both puzzled and embarrassed by her attitude, although later I realized that it just reflected her nature, which was strictly prosaic. She read a lot about history and travel and was fond of whatever revealed the nature of daily life in the past, for example the letters of Horace Walpole, Mrs Delany and Madame de Sévigné (she almost knew by heart several of de Sévigné's), but language used for its beauty, not to convey information, meant little to her, and she preferred to look outwards rather than inwards. Indeed I think that writing about emotions appeared to her rather indecent, and certainly unnecessary.

My father, on the other hand, loved poetry and thoroughly enjoyed Shakespeare, which was lucky for me. I am nearly as prosaic as my mother, but I did inherit enough of his disposition to prevent me from going as far in that direction as she did. He saved Shakespeare for me, and a good deal more. However, when someone asks me for my favourite poem and I answer Lear's 'The Owl and the Pussy Cat', I am not being facetious. I really do prefer poems which tell a story to those that plumb the depths of experience, and those that depend largely on associations hooked up into a poet's mind by words and images are lost to me. I read to see something, not to decipher codes.

People sometimes ask writers what book first inspired and helped to shape them. I find that a hard question to answer. I learnt to read early and can't remember a birthday or Christmas when my presents did not consist of books, so it is impossible for me to imagine how I would have developed without them and can safely say that they did much to shape me. But did any one of them jolt me alive? Not that I can remember. There were many good children's books – all loved, except those in which I could detect a whiff of do-gooding – followed by generous dollops of romance, before I reached the classics via the Brontës and Jane Austen, whereupon the world opened up ... And there is one writer whose words about writing are always with me: Jean Rhys. She hardly ever talked about it, and when she did it was in the simplest way possible: 'I have to try to get it *like it really was*' and 'You can't cut too much'. Those words have done a lot to keep me in order, but I can't say that they inspired me.

The two great writers I think about most often I love for their personalities rather than their artistry – and do so in spite of the fact that I am glad that I never had to meet them: James Boswell, and Byron. Boswell I love for his journals, not for his portrait of Dr Johnson, marvellous though that is, and Byron for his letters, more even than for *Don Juan*.

What is irresistible about Boswell is his always wanting with passionate intensity to be a good man and making stern resolutions to that end, almost never failing to break those resolutions, and then recording this process with fascinated honesty, as though he were a naturalist recording the behaviour of some strange creature. The one time he managed to maintain goodness for several months was when his father got him to study law in what was, to him, boring, boring, *boring* Utrecht by promising him a tour of Europe if he kept it up. It was a fearful struggle, but he kept sober, he managed (just) not to fuck whores, he very rarely made a fool of himself by talking too much at parties – and it brought him to the edge of a nervous breakdown; he feared, in anguished passages in his journal, that he was going mad. But it was worth it: the subsequent Grand Tour was bliss. In Naples he likened himself to a lion 'running after girls without restraint', and in beautiful Sienna 'to enjoy was the thing. Intoxicated by that sweet delirium I gave myself up, without self-reproach and in complete serenity, to the charms of irregular love.'

He became a good lawyer and he had the sense to end his series of elaborate campaigns to secure a rich wife, to which a whole volume of the journals is devoted, by marrying his sensible and far from rich cousin Margaret because they loved each other. She, knowing him well, would not have loved him, and neither would Dr Johnson, who did not suffer fools gladly, if Boswell had not had charm and (for all his absurdities) intelligence beyond the ordinary. Of course he did: his writing sparkles with it. And there is also, whatever he is getting up to, an engaging underlying guilelessness about him.

That was not a quality shared by Byron, although the direction taken by his career was largely determined by immaturity. He was, in a sense, 'self-made'. He never knew his father, had good reason to find his mother impossible, and was afflicted with a club foot, a deformity which he found humiliating, so it is not surprising that he had a tendency to skid into depression. Having a vast amount of imaginative energy and intelligence, he built himself a defiantly brilliant personality, and did it so successfully that to this day the adjective 'Byronic' means 'extremely, even dangerously romantic'. People forget, therefore, how young he was when he became famous overnight at the age of twenty-four with the publication of *Childe Harold*. Even when he died at the age of thirty-six he had not yet reached his full potential, though he had advanced far enough towards it to suggest a truly impressive future.

His letters show that he first met Augusta, his half-sister, when he was a schoolboy, and that she meant a great deal to him at once, because here at last was someone *belonging to him*. She knew what he meant when he complained about his mother, something he couldn't decently do to anyone else. They could giggle together. And later, of course, it became evident that she had the quality he enjoyed most in a woman: cosiness. The women Byron was happiest with were always the cosy ones: Augusta; Lady Oxford, with her brood of children by miscellaneous fathers, with whom he had a delightfully trouble-free affair; the first of his Venetian mistresses; and finally Teresa, Contessa Guiccioli. That Teresa was something of a goose and Augusta very much of one mattered not at all. Byron was able to appreciate intelligent women, but preferred to do it from a distance; for close-up he much preferred a goose to a bluestocking.

He went into his disastrous marriage because he did not yet fully know himself, and accepted the worldly wisdom of Lady Melbourne, his mother substitute. He was terribly short of money, and to her the solution was obvious: he must stop inviting trouble by messing about with his half-sister (which was making him feel guilty anyway) and marry a rich woman. Because he was so clever, Lady Melbourne may have thought that Anne Isabella Milbanke's celebrated intellect would suit him! So there he was, tied to a woman who was not only a bit of a bluestocking but also smugly determined to save his soul. It was a dreadful mistake which inflamed his tendency to depression and drove him almost at once into uncharacteristic hysteria and cruelty. His own belief was that his romantic poetry was a safety valve which saved him from going mad, which was why he always insisted that he was not proud of it (he said this in his private diary as well as publicly). This crisis, however, was beyond solution by verse. It propelled him into exile, from which he was to send some of the best letters ever written.

They are so good because he (like Boswell) wrote as he spoke, at a time when people usually adopted a formal and supposedly more elegant style when they put pen to paper. You can clearly hear his voice, so the many years between him and you shrivel away. Witty, often flippant, kind and generous, sometimes rather comically showing-off, sometimes shrewd, honest, always acutely *alive*, there he is, the man who wrote that marvellous poem *Don Juan*. How extraordinary – how wonderful! – it is that a lot of little black marks on paper can bring a person who died nearly two hundred years ago into your room: bring him so close that you know him much better than you would have known him if you met him in the flesh. It is extraordinary and it is *enlarging*. When I had to get rid of most of my books in order to fit in the little room that is now my home, there was never any doubt that Boswell and Byron would have to come with me.

Dead Right

Back in the 1920s my mother never went to a funeral if she could help it, and was horrified when she heard of children being exposed to such an ordeal, and my father vanished from the room if death was mentioned; and very much later, in the 1960s, when the publishers where I was a partner brought out a beautiful and amusing book about the trappings of death, booksellers refused to stock something so 'morbid'. I was born in December 1917, so was fully immersed in this refusal to contemplate death. Indeed it was not until over thirty years later, when I had to visit a coroner's office to identify a woman who had been found dead, that I thought for the first time how extraordinary – indeed how ridiculous – it was to have lived for so long without ever having seen a dead body. I have heard it suggested that this recoil from the subject was a result of the First World War filling everyone's minds with an acute and appalled awareness of death, but my own explanation was, and still is, that it was a pendulum-swing away from the preceding century's obsession with the subject – the relish for mourning, ranging from solemn viewing of the corpse by young and old alike, to passionate concern about the exact degree of blackness to be worn, and how long for (for the rest of your days if you were a widow). A mood so extreme surely had to result in a strong reaction.

It seems to me that what influences the consciousness in wartime is not death. It is killing. And no, they are not the same thing.

Death is the inevitable end of an individual object's existence – I don't say 'end of life' because it is a part of life. Everything begins, develops, if animal or vegetable, breeds, then fades away: *everything*, not just humans, animals, plants, but things which seem to us eternal, such as rocks. Mountains wear down from jagged peaks to flatness. Even planets decay. That natural process is death. Killing is the obscene intervention of violence, the violation which prevents a human being or any other animal from reaching death as it should be reached. Killing certainly did affect the minds of those exposed to it by the First World War. It shocked most of them into silence: many of the men who survived fighting in it never spoke of it, and I think it had the same effect on most of those the men returned to. It was too dreadful. They shut down on it.

My maternal grandparents' house, in which the children of my generation spent all their holidays, and where we stayed if our empire-serving parents were abroad in some place inhospitable to the young, was typical of those times in that the only music-making objects in it were an upright piano and a small wind-up record player that had belonged to my uncle when he was a boy – something probably unthinkable to children today. There was no pop music because there were no teenagers, only children and grown-ups. Certainly once the children had turned twelve they began being restive (the grown-ups called it 'the awkward age') but there was little to be done about it. There were music-hall songs and dance music, but they could only come into a home via sheet music and if there was someone there who could play the piano, and the limit of adult piano-playing in our family was nursery rhymes to amuse the little ones. A hint of the future might have been detected in the eagerness with which we children fell on Uncle Billy's little 'gramophone', which had been forgotten about by the grown-ups. We listened over and over again to the few records that went with it – some Gilbert and Sullivan songs and two or three spirituals sung by Paul Robeson. Right at the back of the cupboard where they lived I once found another record, which turned out to be a wartime song, a comic and rather witty version of 'Who Killed Cock Robin' called 'Who Killed Bill Kaiser'. Although I was born before the war's end, it was as remote and unreal to me as the Wars of the Roses, so I was as thrilled as I would have been if I had dug up a medieval helmet, and ran to show the record to my mother. All she said was, 'That old thing – is it still there?' It was a shock to come up so suddenly against the fact that what to me was history, to her was just something from the day before yesterday. Absolutely no trace of that day before yesterday had been injected into my consciousness by my elders, so whatever I was to feel about death, it had nothing to do with war.

My own experience of the Second World War confirmed this. Before it started, during the horrible months when we could all feel it coming, I said to a friend: 'If it does start I think I'll kill myself.' (Although the preceding war had been little talked about, poets and novelists had written about it, so we were fully aware that a repetition ought to be unthinkable.) My friend replied, 'Killing yourself to avoid being killed would be a bit silly,' and I felt sadly that she was being obtuse. It was not the prospect of being killed that was distressing me; it was having to know this obscenity about life. And that, not fear of death, was what polluted one's consciousness all through the war, so that the moment it was over we too shut down on it.

Because we did shut down. 'IT'S OVER!' That knowledge wiped out any other feeling. I could see no reason to be anything but happy, and death was just something that would occur when I was old – and which was not, and never had been, frightening.

That this was true, I owe to Montaigne. I can't remember when I read, or was told, that he considered it a good thing to spend a short time every day thinking about death, thus getting used to its inevitability and coming to understand that something inevitable is natural and can't be too bad, but it was in my early teens, and it struck me as a sensible idea. Of course I didn't set out to think about death in a regular way every day, but I did think about it quite often, and sure enough, it worked. Why coming to see death's naturalness should have caused belief in an afterlife to melt away, I am unsure, but it did. Probably that belief had been no more than an unexamined acceptance of something said by a grown-up: in a child's life there are many things more important to question than the probability of reuniting after death with other dead people – an idea that is tucked away on a back shelf of the mind like some object for which one has no use at present.

When I was sixteen I had my appendix removed: an operation common in those days, which seems to have gone out of fashion. Going under the anaesthetic, which was chloroform, caused an interesting confrontation with that particular idea. As a little girl I had occasionally suspected that there was a monster under my bed waiting to come out and get me, scaring myself so much that I had to be calmed down and assured that I was imagining it. Presumably the anaesthetist preparing me for the operation diminished the flow of chloroform too soon, because I became conscious, without the least idea of where I was or what was happening: all I knew was that I was lying on my back, on a bed, with a stifling claw clamped down on my face. *They had been lying!* The monster had been there all the time and now it had come out and got me, I was dying! The dying felt like tipping over the edge of a cliff into black nothingness. I was hanging desperately on to the rim of the cliff. I was staring into that black nothingness – and, horror of horrors, understood that it was *not* nothingness: there were shapes swimming about, things happening, creatures at large out there and I was about to be pitched in amongst all that, unprepared, ignorant, totally incapable of coping. It was terrifying – surely one was supposed to change in some way at death, but I was still unchanged, still just my miserably inadequate self . . . Into my mind there came the thought, 'If I start to believe in God perhaps I'll be allowed to change so that I will know what to do?' At which (and I'm still proud of this) I answered myself: 'No! That would be too shameful, just because I'm frightened.' I let go, and down into the black nothingness I slid.

So: when many years later I really was near death as a result of haemorrhage after my miscarriage, and understood as much quite clearly, I was not alarmed. My last thought – if that had turned out to be what it was – would have been acceptance.

And now I live in an old people's home with forty-two others, our average age being ninety, or perhaps a little more. When one makes the difficult decision (and difficult it is) to retire from normal life, get rid of one's home and most of one's possessions, and move into such a place (or be moved, which doesn't apply here, I am glad to say), it means that one has reached the stage of thinking, 'How am I going to manage my increasing incompetence now that I'm so old? Who is going to look after me when I can no longer look after myself?' Death is no longer something in the distance, but might well be encountered any time now. You might suppose that this would make it more alarming, but judging from what I now see around me, the opposite happens. Being within sight, it has become something for which one ought to prepare. One of the many things I like about my retirement home is the sensible, practical attitude towards death that prevails here. You are asked without embarrassment whether you would rather die here or in a hospital, whether you want to be kept alive whatever happens or would prefer a heart attack, for instance, to be allowed to take its course, and how you wish your body to be disposed of. When a death occurs in the home it is dealt with with the utmost respect – and also with a rather amazing tact in relation to us, the survivors: I doubt whether anyone has ever been aware of a death at the moment of its happening, or of the removal of a body, which must involve very careful management.

These matters have become discussable with one's friends, not, of course, as a frequent part of daily gossip over lunch in the dining room, which is our only communal occasion, but from time to time, and I am pretty sure that most of us here would consider it silly to be frightened of being dead. All of us, however, feel some degree of anxiety about *the process of dying.*

That process depends on what you are dying of. The body can fail in ways that are extremely distressing, slowly and painfully, demanding much stoicism, or it can switch off with little more than a flash of dizziness. In my family we seem to have been uncommonly lucky in that respect. There was the eighty-two-year-old uncle who was at a meet of the Norwich Stag Hounds, enjoying a drink with friends, when crash! and he fell off his horse, dead. There was the cousin in her eighties who fell dead as she was filling a kettle to make tea, and the other cousin, ninety-eight, who slipped away so gently that the sister who was holding her hand didn't realize that she had stopped breathing. There was my mother, a week before her ninety-sixth birthday, who had one nasty day, which, to my relief, she couldn't remember the next morning, then slept her way out after speaking her last words, 'It was absolutely divine,' about a recent drive to a beloved place. My father, alas, had a whole week of unhappiness after a blood vessel in his brain had ruptured. He looked up as one came through the door, obviously about to greet one, then when he found he couldn't speak, his expression became one of pain and puzzlement: he understood that something was badly amiss but he didn't know what it was. The moment of his dying, however, was sudden and painless. My brother was the only person near me who clearly resented death, and that was because he had achieved a way of life which suited him so perfectly that he wanted more. He was not frightened of it. 'No one after eighty has any right to complain about death,' he had said to me not long before.

That fortunate record makes me believe that although it would be unwise to *expect* an easy dying, it is not unreasonable to *hope* for one.

As for after it, I feel quite strongly that I would like my ashes to be scattered or buried in a place I love. (I scattered my mother's in her garden – and the old man who tended it for her when she could no longer do it herself said, 'Cor! That won't half make the flowers grow.') But such a feeling, though strong, is really absurd, because what does it matter to the dead how their bodies are disposed of? It is for the mourners to do what suits them best.

A little while ago I took part in a television programme about death that was designed by the photographer Rankin, to help him overcome his fear of it, to which he bravely admitted. Whether it served his purpose or not I don't know – possibly not, because that fear is brewed in the guts, not in the mind – and I remember a man I once knew who suffered from it so badly that he told me he used to wake up in the night and have to telephone his sister and beg her to come round. 'What did she do?' I asked, and he said she made tea and talked sense, but it didn't do much good because the thought of all those bloody silly birds still twittering and those bastards walking up and down the street when he wasn't there to see them drove him mad. But even if Rankin's programme failed to make him feel better, which I hope was not the case, it was excellent, and many viewers responded to it with enthusiasm. I had already understood from the response to my own book, *Somewhere Towards the End*, that the taboo on the subject of death, so heavy in my youth, was evaporating, and the programme was a striking example of how true this is. Even teenagers joined willingly in discussion of it.

The contributor I remember with the most pleasure is the man who said that not existing for thousands and thousands of years before his birth had never worried him for a moment, so why should going back into non-existence at his death cause him dismay? Everyone laughed when he said that and so did I, and as I laughed I thought: 'Dead right!'

What Is

A full moon in a clear sky, waking me
to a far-away time, a far-away space
existing above or under the familiar –
or interwoven with it: a place
of dust-grey deserts, mountains of eroded rock,
turned by being so far away into
a silver disc
floating there to mock
stories of gods, myths of origin, hell's penalties
or heaven's bliss;
saying Look!
Why want anything more marvellous
than what is.

D.A. 17.3.10

Acknowledgements

Although in some ways you become more confident with old age – stop minding, for example, what other people think – in others you become less so. As I advanced through my nineties I became increasingly unsure of my own abilities. 'Will you write another book?' people asked, and the answer was I couldn't. I still enjoyed writing and could easily bring off a book review or short article for a newspaper, but a book? No. The first person I have to thank in relation to *Alive, Alive Oh!* is Pru Rowlandson, a friend since I was first published by Granta, where she managed (as she still does) their publicity. I forget her exact words, but they amounted to 'You could at least have a go at it.' I suppose I could, thought I, so I did. Thank you, Pru.

Once a lot of written pages had appeared, doubt re-awoke.

Could they be called *a book*? I needed the opinion of an outsider, someone book-wise but who didn't know or care about *me*. Pru suggested Rebecca Carter. 'Of course it's a book,' she said, 'and I love it' – which was a happy moment. She is now my agent. Thank you, Rebecca.

I must now confess that, having spent a working lifetime as a publisher's editor, I had never supposed that I myself might need an editor. There was a moment, after Granta had made an offer for *Alive, Alive Oh!* when – I blush to remember this – I bristled slightly at the suggestion that Bella Lacey should edit it. What I had forgotten during my post-publishing years was that the one person who really loves a good editor is – the author! Here is someone giving your precious book one hundred per cent of expert attention (something, believe it or not, very few books ever get however popular they become) and who is doing so in order to discover those moments (few you hope, but there are always some) when it happens to fall just a little short of your intention. Her or his job is to make your book *even more yours* (I have said we are speaking of a *good* editor). Thank you, Bella.

Whatever happens to this book in the future, the above three people made the writing of it a great pleasure.